I Am a Cat

SŌSEKI NATSUME

I Am a Cat

translated by
Aiko Itō and Graeme Wilson

CHARLES E. TUTTLE CO.
Rutland/Vermont & Tokyo/Japan

Originally published in Japan by the Asahi Shimbun
Publishing Company in the *Japan Quarterly*, Vol. XVII
No. 4 and Vol. XVIII Nos. 1 and 2

Published by the Charles E. Tuttle Company, Inc.
an imprint of Periplus Editions (HK) Ltd.

ISBN 0-8048-1621-2

First printing, 1972
Twenty-eighth printing, 1999
Printed in Singapore

Distribution:

North America
 Tuttle Publishing
 Distribution Center
 Airport Industrial Park
 364 Innovation Drive
 North Clarendon, VT 05759-9436
 Tel: (802) 773-8930
 Tel: (800) 526-2778

Japan
 Tuttle Publishing
 RK Building 2nd Floor
 2-13-10 Shimo-Meguro, Meguro-Ku
 Tokyo 153-0064
 Tel: (03) 5437-0171
 Fax: (03) 5437-0755

Asia Pacific
 Berkeley Books Pte. Ltd.
 5 Little Road #08-01
 Singapore 536983
 Tel: (65) 280-3320
 Fax: (65) 280-6290

Introduction

NATSUME SŌSEKI is the pen name of Natsume Kin'nosuke (1867–1916), the eighth and youngest son of an hereditary ward-chief in Tokyo under the Tokugawa shogunate. Such *nanushi*, though privileged to the point of being minor town-gentry, were not *samurai*. His father's post disappeared with the collapse of the Tokugawa shogunate and the Meiji Restoration of 1868, and the family thus fell upon hard times made yet harder by that gay improvidence which was, and still is, regarded as right conduct by the citizens of Tokyo. Sōseki received the compulsory modern education, both primary and at middle school level, which had been introduced in 1872; but his teachers had, of course, themselves been trained in precisely that Chinese classical tradition by which his own childhood had been conditioned. "When I was a boy," he later wrote, "I could recite thousands of lines of T'ang and Sung poetry"; and he always preferred the hard plangency of *bungotai*, the traditional literary language derived from Chinese models, to the smoother, almost feminine, characteristics of ordinary Japanese.

In his mid-teens he switched to a private school for Chinese studies and, though upper-class tradition regarded literature as no more than a civilized diversion, he began to toy with the idea of adopting it as a working profession. Realizing that Chinese studies were anachronistic and would probably prove financially unrewarding at a time when Japan was avidly absorbing "Western enlightenment," he next considered becoming an architect. At all events he determined to enter a university, for which purpose he studied to acquire the prerequisite knowledge of English ("which I hate").

In 1881, in pursuit of his architectural ambition (and he had some real talent as a draftsman and painter) he entered the junior course of the engineering department at Tokyo Imperial University, then the only university in the capital; but he changed the same year to the department of literature and in 1890, somewhat oddly in the light of his earlier remarks, he decided to specialize in English and entered the English literature department of the university.

The English department, founded in 1888, had only produced one previous graduate, a student of the first year who became a customs inspector in Shanghai. Sōseki graduated in July 1893 and then

briefly enrolled as a postgraduate student.
He applied unsuccessfully for a post with
the English-language *Japan Mail* in Yokohama and taught for a time at Tokyo
Normal College. In 1895 he suddenly left
Tokyo to become a provincial teacher,
first in Shikoku (where his university
friend, the *haiku* poet Masaoka Shiki, re-
sided) and later, in 1896, at Kumamoto in
Kyushu: there, by formal arrangement, he
married the eldest daughter of the chief
secretary of the House of Peers.

In 1900 the Ministry of Education sent
him on a miserable scholarship to London
University. Living in a succession of ever
cheaper digs (of which No. 6, Flodden
Road, Camberwell was a not untypical
example), he seems to have done nothing
but read an almost incredible number of
books on every conceivable subject. His
only social contacts with the British appear
to have been a weekly private English
lesson with W. J. Craig, subsequently the
editor of the *Arden Shakespeare*, and a
single tea party given in Dulwich by the
wife of a missionary whom he had met on
the ship bringing him to England. It is,
therefore, perhaps not surprising that Sōseki formed a poor opinion of English
social life and that in Japan he was widely
rumored to have gone mad.

In 1903 he returned to Tokyo and, in
fulfillment of the terms of his London
scholarship, served four years as a lecturer

in English literature (succeeding Lafcadio Hearn) at Tokyo Imperial University. During this period he began writing. He had formed various useful literary friendships while he was a student at the university, and, though his close friend Shiki had died in 1902, the editorial board of the influential literary magazine *Hototogisu* (*Cuckoo*), which Shiki had founded, still included men who were either Sōseki's personal friends or otherwise well disposed toward the bright young man who had just taken over Lafcadio Hearn's lectureship.

One of these editors, Takahama Kyoshi, allegedly asked Sōseki to write something for the magazine. Accordingly, during 1904, Sōseki produced his first short story, which he called *I Am a Cat*. Takahama read it, told Sōseki that it was no good, and, when Sōseki asked for an explanation, provided comment in considerable detail. Today it seems ludicrous that one of the three or four best novelists ever to write in Japanese should have been glad to receive guidance from such a relatively insignificant figure as Takahama, whose main claim, *sub specie aeternitatis,* to literary notice is that he used his editorship to support those haiku-writers who, scared of the freedoms implicit in Shiki's revitalization of the haiku, sought to maintain in the strictest form all the paralysing rigidities of its traditional conventions. But it must be remembered that, at that time, Takahama was a well-known, well-established and very influential editor (a man with the sensitivity to divine Sōseki's promise and the kindness to give him guidance), while Sōseki was a virtually unknown young man who had just produced his first, and really rather odd, short story. At all events, Sōseki appears to have accepted the advice (though he later stated that he could not remember what that advice had been) and rewrote the story. Takahama liked the second version and published it in the January 1905 issue of *Hototogisu.*

Sōseki had not intended to write more than that single short story which is now the first chapter of a very long book, but Takahama was so pleased with its immediate success that he persuaded Sōseki to write further installments. The subsequent ten chapters were thus successively published in *Hototogisu's* issues for February, April, June, July and October 1905 and for January, March, April and August 1906. The seventh and eighth chapters appeared together in the issue for January 1906. This somewhat curious account of the origin and development of Sōseki's famous novel rests primarily upon Takahama's testimony in his later book *Sōseki and I,* but there is no reason to doubt that it is substantially correct. The actual book was first published in three-volume form, the volumes appearing in October 1905, November 1906 and May 1907. The first single-volume edition was published in 1911.

Takahama's account explains the unevenness, even jerkiness, of the early parts of the book. Indeed, though the first chapter is adequately articulated into the total work, it is as clear from that chapter's ending as from Sōseki's own later remarks ("When the first chapter appeared in *Hototogisu*, it was my intention to stop there") that he originally meant to write no more. There are, moreover, one or two minor points in that first chapter which an ungenerous critic might highlight as inconsistent with subsequent portions of the book. The second chapter, nearly the longest of them all, shows Sōseki still feeling his way towards the right chapter length. He did not really hit his stride until the third chapter, which finally established the tone, length and character of the remaining eight.

The circumstances of the book's construction no doubt largely account for its rambling structure and discursive content; but Sōseki must very quickly have realized that the technique used by Sterne for the construction of *The Life and Opinions of Tristram Shandy* would very neatly solve his own problems. Though Sōseki's total book is held together by the continuing theme of a nameless cat's observations on upper-middle-class Japanese society of the Meiji period, the essence of the book resides in the humor and the sardonic truth of those various observations, not in the development of the story. The cat's eventual drunken death in a water-butt comes without any particular reason or structural build-up, and one is forced to the conclusion that Sōseki simply drowned his hero because he had run out of sufficiently humorous observations to offer on Meiji society.

It is consequently possible to take almost any single chapter of the book as an isolated short story. In presenting the first three chapters in this present book, we are following the pattern set by one of Sōseki's most eminent pupils, Komiya Toyotaka, whose selections from Sōseki's total literary production, published by Kaizōsha in their 1927 series *Gendai Nihon Bungaku Zenshū* (*Collection of Modern Japanese Literature*), included the first three chapters of *I Am a Cat* as best representative of Sōseki's first and perhaps most famous book.

Sōseki wrote several other books while at the university, notably *Botchan* (a satire reflecting his teaching experience at Shikoku), but he disliked university life and, rightly, considered himself very poorly paid. He accordingly resigned as soon as he could (1907) and became the literary editor of the *Asahi Shimbun*. He continued in that journal's employment, publishing several novels as serials in its pages, until his death in 1916 from complications arising from those stomach troubles which plagued the last ten years of his life.

* * *

Natsume Sōseki is generally recognized in Japan as the best writer of prose to have emerged during the century since contact was re-established with the outside world in 1868. His only possible rival, Tanizaki Junichirō, writes with rather less assurance in the total propriety of Japanese: his prose reflects his early fascination by the West. Sōseki's deep scholarship both in Chinese and in English literature eminently qualified him for that marrying of Eastern and Western traditions which was the declared objective of Meiji policy-makers. Unlike the majority of his contemporaries who had learned their English in mission schools, Sōseki approached Western literature with the wary sensitivity of a man deep-versed in the Chinese tradition. He was thus in no way overawed by his English studies. He was, of course, also deep-versed in Japanese literature, but his mature work shows little of its influence except in those rather poor *haiku* for which

he once had a very considerable reputation. It should, however, be remembered
that he himself sharply criticized Shiki's
haiku for their obsession with form and
their neglect of substance; a criticism
striking at the heart of all *haiku*.

The main Japanese influences upon his
writing were, oddly enough in a man of
gentle birth, those *rakugo*, comic recita-
tions by professional storytellers, to which
his childhood circle had been addicted. The
rakugo techniques are especially noticeable
in his masterly use of dialogue. It is also
worth stressing that, though his Chinese
studies resulted in a style as concise as that
literary language traditionally employed in
the composition of *tanka* and *haiku*, much
of the vitality of his prose writing derives
from his skilled exploitation of colloquial
Japanese speech (*kōgotai*).

Indeed, Sōseki's writing represents a
continuation into modern times of that
city-culture which first flowered in the late
17th century when the wealth of the towns
prospering under the *Pax Tokugawa* provided the economic base for an urban
and specifically non-aristocratic literature.
Critics have often contrasted Sōseki's ra-
tionalist and (in the best sense) liberal out-
look with the rigid *samurai* attitudes of his
great contemporary, Mori Ōgai (1862–
1922), all of whose attitudes including his
literary opinions were precisely those

which one might expect from a surgeon general in the Imperial Japanese Army. Which Ōgai was. On one occasion Sōseki complained (an interesting complaint from the point of view of the English who regard themselves as simultaneously monarchist and democratic) that Jonathan Swift in *Gulliver's Travels* showed far too much concern with kings and courts. The Japanese comment upon Sōseki's remark was that it would never have been made by Mori Ōgai. Another story illustrating Sōseki's untraditional independence of thought and attitude is that which tells of him voicing objections when, at a Nō performance where smoking was prohibited, the Empress was seen to be puffing away. No doubt Ōgai would have proffered ashtrays.

Sōseki's longer novels reflect his assiduous study of the construction and mechanisms of the English novel and, in particular, his liking for the works of Laurence Sterne, Jonathan Swift and Jane Austen. He shared their sly ironic turn of mind, and their influence on his work was more deep and lasting than that, so frequently cited by contemporary critics, of George Meredith. Without impugning Sōseki's real originality, it is fair to point out that the methods used to delineate character and to highlight (without deriding) foible are the same in *I Am a Cat* and *Tristram*

Shandy. Sterne's wry self-portraiture is echoed in Sōseki's, though the latter has more obviously distributed aspects of his own nature among several characters in his book.

It is also worth stressing the apparent oddity of choosing for the main character in one's first published writing a stray kitten, and a stray kitten world-weary from the moment of its birth. But as soon as he was born, Sōseki's parents had put him out to nurse. In his first year he was adopted by the Shiobara family. He only rejoined his own family when the Shiobaras were divorced some eight years later. And even then he only learned that his parents were his parents from the whisperings of servants. Sōseki, was, in fact, himself a stray kitten; and he lived his life as do all those who feel themselves born middle-aged.

For the most part, the main figures in all his novels are male intellectuals; and the strong traditionalist element in his make-up (of which his *haiku* were a by-product) included an extremely old-fashioned attitude toward women. It is recorded that his first words to his wife were "I am a scholar, and must therefore study. I have no time to fuss over you. Please understand this clearly." His anti-feminism, which is lightly foreshadowed in his portraits of all the females (except the she-cat Tortoiseshell) in the first three chapters of *I Am a Cat*, emerges very plainly in *Gubijinsō* (*Poppy*), the fourth of his thirteen novels, which appeared in 1907. But his last and uncompleted work, *Meian* (*Light and Darkness*) of 1916, shows a complete change of attitude: the book's main character is a newly married wife whose problems are analyzed with real understanding and warm sympathy. It seems likely that this development in his writing reflected a parallel development in his own personal life.

* * *

There is an understandable tendency for critics of any literature to emphasize the dependence of a writer on his predecessors, but the "game of influences" is all too frequently played with an enthusiasm which leads to an unfair disregard of the writer's real originality. So far as Japan is concerned, there can be no doubt whatever that Sōseki's originality was a main factor in his popular success; but he also has genuine claims to originality in world literature. World literature has, of course, a long tradition of animal-fables, animal-myths and major groupings of stories around such figures as Renard the Fox and even Brer Rabbit. But Sōseki's device of dealing with a human world through animal eyes appears to be entirely original.

Sōseki's modernity is even more strikingly illustrated by the fact that sixty years ago the characters in *I Am a Cat* (notably "the aesthete") were all fully engaged in those comic ploys and counter-ploys of gamesmanship, lifemanship and one-upmanship which are now usually associated with the comparatively recent work of Stephen Potter. The passages in the first chapter of *I Am a Cat* about Gibbon's *History of the French Revolution* and Harrison's *Theophano* are both extremely fine examples of what Potter has called "rilking." Similarly, the description of the visit to a restaurant in the second chapter is a particularly well-developed example of Potter's comic techniques.

Perhaps the most significant aspect of Sōseki's work is that, while deeply conversant with Western literature and while sharply and persistently critical of Japanese society, he remained unswamped (even, perhaps, unimpressed) by Western enlightenment. Throughout his career he remained essentially and uncompromisingly Japanese; and his deadly serious attitude is, typically, revealed in that comic, even coarse, account in *Koto no Sorane* (1905) of the protest by Japanese badgers against contemporary Japanese infatuation with routine badger-tricks (such as the "hypnotic method") whose sole novelty is that their names have been exported to Japan by "badgers in the West." Probably for this reason Sōseki's writings have retained their popularity and, perhaps, even extended their influence. In a recent public opinion survey conducted by the *Asahi Shimbun* among students and professors at four universities which still produce the social and intellectual élite of Japan, Sōseki's *Kokoro* (*The Heart of Things*) of 1914 was second only to Dostoievski's *Crime and Punishment* in the list of books which had most influenced the thinking of the interviewees. *Yukiguni* (*Snow Country*) by Nobel Prize winner Kawabata Yasunari was seventeenth.

* * *

Sōseki's brilliant and extremely concise use of the Japanese language makes all his writings difficult to translate. In the case of this particular book, difficulty arises with the very first word of its title, *Wagahai wa Neko de Aru*. There being no English equivalent for the Japanese word *Wagahai*, the main significance of that title, the comic incongruity of a mere cat, a mere stray mewling kitten, referring to itself in so lordly a manner, cannot be conveyed to the English reader. That kind of difficulty (and there are many others, notably those arising from Sōseki's extraordinarily wide

range of idiomatic reference) inevitably
recurs in the subsequent quarter-million
words. Such problems usually lead translators to beg the indulgence of their readers: but forgive them not, for they know
what they do.

—THE TRANSLATORS

I AM A CAT. As yet I have no name. I've no idea where I was born. All I remember is that I was miaowing in a dampish dark place when, for the first time, I saw a human being. This human being, I heard afterwards, was a member of the most ferocious human species; a *shosei*, one of those students who, in return for board and lodging, perform small chores about the house. I hear that, on occasion, this species catches, boils and eats us. However as at that time I lacked all knowledge of such creatures, I did not feel particularly frightened. I simply felt myself floating in the air as I was lifted up lightly on his palm. When I accustomed myself to that position, I looked at his face. This must have been the very first time that ever I set eyes on a human being. The impression of oddity which I then received still remains today. First of all, the face that should be decorated with hair is as bald as a kettle. Since that day I have met many a cat but never have I come across such deformity. The center of the face protrudes excessively and sometimes, from the holes in that protuberance, smoke comes out in little puffs. I was originally somewhat troubled by such exhalations for they made me choke, but I learnt only recently that it was the smoke of burnt tobacco which humans like to breathe.

For a little while I sat comfortably in that creature's palm, but things soon developed at a tremendous speed. I could not tell whether the *shosei* was in movement or whether it was only I that moved; but anyway I began to grow quite giddy, to feel sick. And just as I was thinking that the giddiness would kill me, I heard a thud and saw a million stars. Thus far I can remember but, however hard I try, I cannot recollect anything thereafter.

When I came to myself, the creature had gone. I had at one time had a basketful of brothers, but now not one could be seen. Even my precious mother had disappeared. Moreover I now found myself in a painfully bright place most unlike that nook where once I'd sheltered. It was in fact so bright that I could hardly keep my eyes open. Sure that there was something wrong, I began to crawl about. Which proved painful. I had been snatched away from softest straw only to be pitched with violence into a prickly clump of bamboo grass.

After a struggle, I managed to scramble clear of the clump and emerged to find a wide pond stretching beyond it. I sat at the edge of the pond and wondered what to do. No helpful thought occurred. After

a while it struck me that, if I cried, perhaps
the *shosei* might come back to fetch me. I
tried some feeble mewing, but no one came.
Soon a light wind blew across the pond and it
began to grow dark. I felt extremely hungry.
I wanted to cry, but I was too weak to do so.
There was nothing to be done. However,
having decided that I simply must find food,
I turned, very very slowly, left around the
pond. It was extremely painful going.
Nevertheless, I persevered and crawled on
somehow till at long last I reached a place
where my nose picked up some trace of
human presence. I slipped into a property
through a gap in a broken bamboo fence,
thinking that something might turn up once
I had got inside. It was sheer chance; if the
bamboo fence had not been broken just at
that point, I might after all have starved to
death at the road-side. I realize now how
true the adage is that what is to be will be.
To this very day that gap has served as my
short-cut to the neighbor's tortoiseshell.

Well, though I had managed to creep into
the property, I had no idea what to do next.
Soon it got really dark. I was hungry, it
was cold and rain began to fall. I could
not afford to lose any more time. I had no
choice but to struggle toward a place which
seemed, since brighter, warmer. I did not
know it then, but I was in fact already inside
the house where now I had a chance to
observe further specimens of human kind.
The first one that I met was O-san, the serv-

ant-woman, one of a species yet more savage than the *shosei*. No sooner had she seen me than she grabbed me by the scruff of the neck and flung me out of the house. Accepting that I had no hope, I lay stone-still, my eyes tight shut and trusting to Providence. But the hunger and the cold were more than I could bear. Seizing a moment when O-san had relaxed her watch, I crawled up once again to flop into the kitchen. I was soon flung out again. I crawled up yet again, only yet again to be flung out. I remember that the process was several times repeated. Ever since that time, I have been utterly disgusted with this O-san person. The other day I managed at long last to rid myself of my sense of grievance, for I squared accounts by stealing her dinner of mackerel-pike. As I was about to be flung out for the last time, the master of the house appeared, complaining of the noise and demanding an explanation. The servant lifted me up, turned my face to the master and said "This little stray kitten is being a nuisance. I keep putting it out and it keeps crawling back into the kitchen." The master briefly studied my face, twisting the black hairs under his nostrils. Then "In that case, let it stay," he said; and turned and went inside. The master seemed to be a person of few words. The servant resentfully threw me down in the kitchen. And it was thus that I came to make this house my dwelling.

My master seldom comes face to face

with me. I hear he is a schoolteacher. As soon as he comes home from school, he shuts himself up in the study for the rest of the day; and he seldom emerges. The others in the house think that he is terribly hard-working. He himself pretends to be hard-working. But actually he works less hard than any of them think. Sometimes I tiptoe to his study for a peep and find him taking a snooze. Occasionally his mouth is drooling onto some book he has begun to read. He has a weak stomach and his skin is of a pale yellowish color, inelastic and lacking in vitality. Nevertheless he is an enormous gormandiser. After eating a great deal, he takes some taka-diastase for his stomach and, after that, he opens a book. When he has read a few pages, he becomes sleepy. He drools onto the book. This is the routine religiously observed each evening. There are times when even I, I a mere cat, can put two thoughts together. "Teachers have it easy. If you are born a human, it's best to become a teacher. For if it's possible to sleep this much and still to be a teacher, why, even a cat could teach." However, according to the master, there's nothing harder than a teacher's life and every time his friends come round to see him, he grumbles on and on.

During my early days in the house, I was terribly unpopular with everyone except the master. Everywhere I was unwelcome, and no one would have anything to do with me. The fact that nobody, even to this day, has given me a name indicates quite clearly how very little they have thought about me. Resigned, I try to spend as much of my time as possible with the master; the man who had taken me in. In the morning, while he reads the newspaper, I jump to curl up on his knees. Throughout his afternoon siesta, I sit upon his back. This is not because I have any particular fondness for the master, but because I have no other choice; no one else to turn to. Additionally, and in the light of other experiments, I have decided to sleep on the boiled-rice container which stays warm through the morning, on the quilted foot-warmer during the evening and out on the veranda when it is fine. But what I find especially agreeable is to creep into the children's bed and snuggle down between them. There are two children, one of five and one of three: they sleep in their own room, sharing a bed. I can always find a space between their bodies, and I manage somehow to squeeze myself quietly in. But if, by great ill-luck, one of the children wakes, then I am in trouble. For the children have nasty natures, especially the younger one. They start to cry out noisily, regardless of the time, even in the middle of the night, shouting "Here's the cat!" Then invariably the neurotic dyspeptic in the next room wakes and comes rushing in. Why, only the other day, my master beat my backside black and blue with a wooden ruler.

Living as I do with human beings, the

more that I observe them, the more I am forced to conclude that they are selfish. Especially those children. I find my bed-mates utterly unspeakable. When the fancy takes them, they hang me upside-down, they stuff my face into a paper-bag, they fling me about, they ram me into the kitchen-range. Furthermore, if I do commit so much as the smallest mischief, the entire household unites to chase me round and persecute me. The other day when I happened to be sharpening my claws on some straw floor-matting, the mistress of the house became so unreasonably incensed that now it is only with the greatest reluctance that she'll even let me enter a matted room. Though I'm shivering on the wooden floor in the kitchen, heartlessly she remains indifferent. Miss Blanche, the white cat who lives opposite and whom I much admire, tells me whenever I see her that there is no living creature quite so heartless as a human. The other day, she gave birth to four beautiful kittens. But three days later, the *shosei* of her house removed all four and tossed them away into the backyard pond. Miss Blanche, having given through her tears a complete account of this event, assured me that, to maintain our own parental love and to enjoy our beautiful family life, we, the cat-race, must engage in total war upon all humans. We have no choice but to exterminate them. I think it is a very reasonable proposition. And the three-colored tom-cat living next door is especially indignant that human beings do not understand the nature of proprietary rights. Among our kind it is taken for granted that he who first finds something, be it the head of a dried sardine or a gray mullet's navel, acquires thereby the right to eat it. And if this rule be flouted, one may well resort to violence. But human beings do not seem to understand the rights of property. Every time we come on something good to eat, invariably they descend and take it from us. Relying on their naked strength, they coolly rob us of things which are rightly ours to eat. Miss Blanche lives in the house of a military man, and the tom-cat's master is a lawyer. But since I live in a teacher's house, I take matters of this sort rather more lightly than they. I feel that life is not unreasonable so long as one can scrape along from day to day. For surely even human beings will not flourish forever. I think it best to wait in patience for the Day of the Cats.

Talking of selfishness reminds me that my master once made a fool of himself by reason of this failing. I'll tell you all about it. First you must understand that this master of mine lacks the talent to be more than average at anything at all; but nonetheless he can't refrain from trying his hand at every-thing and anything. He's always writing *haiku* and submitting them to *Cuckoo*: he sends off new-style poetry to *Morning Star*: he has a shot at English prose peppered with gross mistakes: he develops a passion for archery: he takes lessons in chanting *Nō* play-texts: and sometimes he devotes himself to making hideous noises with a violin. But I am sorry to say that none of these activities has led to anything whatever. Yet, though he is dyspeptic, he gets terribly keen once he has embarked upon a project. He once got himself nicknamed "The Maestro of the Water-closet" through chanting in the lavatory, but he remains entirely unconcerned and can still be heard there chanting "I am Taira-no-Munemori." We all say "There goes Munemori" and titter at his antics. I do not know why it happened, but one fine day (a pay-day roughly four weeks after I'd taken up residence) this master of mine came hurrying home with a large parcel under his arm. I wondered what he'd bought. It turned out that he'd purchased water-color paints, brushes and some special "Whatman" paper. It looked to me as if *haiku*-writing and mediaeval chanting were going to be abandoned in favor of water-color painting. Sure enough, from the next day on and every day for some long time, he did nothing but paint pictures in his study. He even went without his afternoon siestas. However, no one could tell what he had painted by looking at the result. Possibly he himself thought little of his work; for one day when his friend who specializes in matters of aesthetics came to visit him, I heard the following conversation.

"Do you know it's quite difficult. When one sees someone else painting, it looks easy enough; but not till one takes a brush oneself, does one realize just how difficult it is." So said my noble master: and it was true enough.

His friend, looking at my master over his gold-rimmed spectacles, observed "It's only natural that one cannot paint particularly well the moment one starts. Besides, one cannot paint a picture indoors by force of the imagination only. The Italian Master, Andrea del Sarto, remarked that if you want to paint a picture, always depict nature as she is. In the sky, there are stars. On earth, there are sparkling dews. Birds are flying. Animals are running. In a pond there are goldfish. On an old tree one sees winter crows. Nature herself is one vast living picture. D'you understand? If you want to paint a picturesque picture, why not try some preliminary sketching?"

"Oh, so Andrea del Sarto said that? I didn't know that at all. Come to think of it, it's quite true. Indeed, it's very true." The master was unduly impressed. I saw a mocking smile behind the gold-rimmed glasses.

The next day when as always I was having a pleasant nap on the veranda, the master emerged from his study (an act unusual in itself) and began behind my back to busy himself with something. At this point I happened to wake up and, wondering what he was up to, opened my eyes just one slit

tenth of an inch. And there he was, fairly
killing himself at being Andrea del Sarto.
I could not help but laugh. He's starting
to sketch me just because he's had his leg
pulled by a friend. I have already slept
enough, and I'm itching to yawn. But
seeing my master sketching away so earnestly,
I hadn't the heart to move: so I bore it all
with resignation. Having drawn my outline,
he's started painting the face. I confess
that, considering cats as works of art, I'm
far from being a collector's piece. I certainly
do not think that my figure, my fur or my
features are superior to those of other cats.
But however ugly I may be, there's no conceivable resemblance between myself and
that queer thing which my master is creating.
First of all, the coloring is wrong. My fur,
like that of a Persian, bears tortoiseshell
markings on a ground of a yellowish pale
grey. It is a fact beyond all argument. Yet
the color which my master has employed is
neither yellow nor black; neither grey nor
brown; nor is it any mixture of those four
distinctive colors. All one can say is that
the color used is a sort of color. Furthermore, and very oddly, my face lacks eyes.
The lack might be excused on the grounds
that the sketch is a sketch of a sleeping cat;
but, all the same, since one cannot find even a
hint of an eye's location, it is not all clear
whether the sketch is of a sleeping cat or of a
blind cat. Secretly I thought to myself that
this would never do, even for Andrea del

Sarto. However, I could not help being struck with admiration for my master's grim determination. Had it been solely up to me, I would gladly have maintained my pose for him, but Nature has now been calling for some time. The muscles in my body are getting pins and needles. When the tingling reached a point where I couldn't stand it another minute, I was obliged to claim my liberty. I stretched my front paws far out in front of me, pushed my neck out low and yawned cavernously. Having done all that, there's no further point in trying to stay still. My master's sketch is spoilt anyway, so I might as well pad round to the backyard and do my business. Moved by these thoughts, I start to crawl sluggishly away. Immediately "You fool" came shouted in my master's voice, a mixture of wrath and disappointment, out of the inner room. He has a fixed habit of saying "You fool" whenever he curses anyone. He cannot help it since he knows no other swear-words. But I thought it rather impertinent of him thus unjustifiably to call me "a fool." After, all I had been very patient up to this point. Of course, had it been his custom to show even the smallest pleasure whenever I jump on his back, I would tamely have endured his imprecations: but it is a bit thick to be called "a fool" just because I get up to go and urinate by someone who has never once with good grace done me a kindness. The prime fact is that all humans are puffed up by their extreme self-satisfaction

with their own brute power. Unless some
creature more powerful than people arrives
on earth to bully them, there's just no knowing to what dire lengths their fool presumptu-
ousness will eventually carry them.

One could put up with this degree of
selfishness, but I once heard a report concerning the unworthiness of humans which is
several times more ugly and deplorable.

At the back of my house there is a small
tea-plantation, perhaps some six yards square.
Though certainly not large, it is a neat and
pleasantly sunny spot. It is my custom to
go there whenever my morale needs strength-
ing; when, for instance, the children are
making so much noise that I cannot doze in
peace or when boredom has disrupted my
digestion. One day, a day of Indian summer, at about two o'clock in the afternoon,
I woke from a pleasant after-luncheon nap
and strolled out to this tea-plantation by
way of taking exercise. Sniffing, one after
another, at the roots of the tea-plants, I came
to the cypress fence at the western end; and
there I saw an enormous cat fast asleep
on a bed of withered chrysanthemums which
his weight had flattened down. He did not
seem to notice my approach. Perhaps he
noticed but did not care. Anyway, there
he was, stretched out at full length and
snoring loudly. I was amazed at the daring
courage which permitted him, a trespasser,
to sleep so unconcernedly in someone else's
garden. He was a pure black cat. The sun

of earliest afternoon was pouring its most brilliant rays upon him, and it seemed as if invisible flames were blazing out from his glossy fur. He had a magnificent physique; the physique, one might say, of the Emperor of Catdom. He was easily twice my size. Filled with admiration and curiosity, I quite forgot myself. I stood stock-still, entranced, all eyes, in front of him. The quiet zephyrs of that Indian summer set gently nodding a branch of Sultan's Parasol which showed above the cypress fence, and a few leaves pattered down upon the couch of crushed chrysanthemums. The Emperor suddenly opened huge round eyes. I remember that moment to this day. His eyes gleamed far more beautifully than that dull amber stuff which humans so inordinately value. He lay dead still. Focussing the piercing light that shone from his eyes' interior upon my dwarfish forehead, he remarked "And who the hell are you?"

I thought his turn of phrase a shade inelegant for an Emperor, but because the voice was deep and filled with a power that could suppress a bulldog, I remained dumbstruck with pure awe. Reflecting, however, that I might get into trouble if I failed to exchange civilities, I answered frigidly, with a false *sang froid* as cold as I could make it, "I, sir, am a cat. I have as yet no name". My heart at that moment was beating a great deal faster than usual.

In a tone of enormous scorn, the Emperor

observed "You...a cat? Well, I'm damned.
Anyway, where the devil do you hang out?"
I thought this cat excessively blunt-spoken.

"I live here, in the teacher's house."

"Huh, I thought as much. 'Orrible scraw-
ny aren't you." Like a true Emperor, he
spoke with great vehemence.

Judged by his manner of speech, he could
not be a cat of respectable background. On
the other hand, he seemed well fed and positively prosperous, almost obese, in his oily
glossiness. I had to ask him "And you, who
on earth are you?"

"Me? I'm Rickshaw Blacky." He gave
his answer with spirit and some pride: for
Rickshaw Blacky is well-known in the
neighborhood as a real rough customer. As
one would expect of those brought up in a
rickshaw-garage, he's tough but quite un-
educated. Hence very few of us mix with
him, and it is our common policy to "keep
him at a respectful distance." Consequently
when I heard his name, I felt a trifle jittery and
uneasy but at the same time a little disdainful
of him. Accordingly, and in order to establish
just how illiterate he was, I pursued the conversation by enquiring. "Which do you think
is superior, a rickshaw-owner or a teacher?"

"Why, a rickshaw-owner, of course. He's
the stronger. Just look at your master, almost skin and bones."

"You, being the cat of a rickshaw-owner,
naturally look very tough. I can see that
one eats well at your establishment."

"Ah well, as far as I'm concerned, I never want for decent grub wherever I go. You too, instead of creeping around in a tea-plantation, why not follow along with me? Within a month, you'd get so fat nobody'd recognize you."

"In due course I might come and ask to join you. But it seems that the teacher's house is larger than your boss's."

"You dim-wit! A house, however big it is, won't help fill an empty belly." He looked quite huffed. Savagely twitching his ears, ears as sharp as slant-sliced stems of the solid bamboo, he took off rowdily.

This was how first I made the acquaintance of Rickshaw Blacky, and since that day I've run across him many times. Whenever we meet he talks big, as might be expected from a rickshaw-owner's cat: but that deplorable incident which I mentioned earlier was a tale he told me.

One day Blacky and I were lying as usual sunning ourselves in the tea-garden. We were chatting about this and that when, having made his usual boasts as if they were all brandnew, he asked me "How many rats have you caught so far?"

While I flatter myself that my general knowledge is wider and deeper than Blacky's, I readily admit that my physical strength and courage are nothing compared with his. All the same, his point-blank question naturally left me feeling a bit confused. Nevertheless, a fact's a fact, and one should face the truth. So I answered "Actually, though I'm always thinking of catching one, I've never yet caught any."

Blacky laughed immoderately, quivering the long whiskers which stuck out stiffly round his muzzle. Blacky, like all true braggarts, is somewhat weak in the head. As long as you purr and listen attentively, pretending to be impressed by his rhodomontade, he is a more or less manageable cat. Soon after getting to know him, I learnt this way to handle him. Consequently on this particular occasion I also thought it would be unwise further to weaken my position by trying to defend myself and that it would be more prudent to dodge the issue by inducing him to brag about his own successes. So without making a fuss, I sought to lead him on by saying "You, judging by your age, must have caught a notable number of rats?" Sure enough, he swallowed the bait with gusto.

"Well, not too many, but I must've caught thirty or forty," was his triumphant answer. "I can cope," he went on, "with a hundred or two hundred rats, any time and by myself. But a weasel, no. That I just can't take. Once I had a hellish time with a weasel."

"Did you really?" I innocently offered. Blacky blinked his saucer eyes but did not discontinue.

"It was last year, the day for the general house-cleaning. As my master was crawling in under the floor-boards with a bag of lime, suddenly a dirty great weasel came whizzing out."

"Really?" I make myself look impressed.

"I say to myself 'So what's a weasel? Only a wee bit bigger than a rat.' So I chase after it, feeling quite excited and finally I got it cornered in a ditch."

"That was well done," I applaud him.

"Not in the least. As a last resort it upped its tail and blew a filthy fart. Ugh! The smell of it! Since that time, whenever I see a weasel, I feel uncommon poorly." At this point, he raised a front paw and stroked his muzzle two or three times as if he were still suffering from last year's stench.

I felt rather sorry for him and, in an effort to cheer him up, said "But when it comes to rats, I expect you just pin them down with one hypnotic glare. And I suppose that it's because you're such a marvelous ratter, a cat well nourished by plenty of rats, that you are so splendidly fat and have such a good complexion." Though this speech was meant to flatter Blacky, strangely enough it had precisely the opposite effect. He looked distinctly cast down and replied with a heavy sigh.

"It's depressing," he said, "when you come to think of it. However hard one slaves at catching rats.... In the whole wide world there's no creature more brazen-faced than a human being. Every rat I catch they confiscate, and they tote them off to the nearest police-box. Since the copper can't tell who caught the rats, he just pays up a penny a tail to anyone that brings them in. My master, for instance, has already earned about half a crown purely through my efforts, but he's never yet stood me a decent meal. The plain fact is that humans, one and all, are merely thieves at heart."

Though Blacky's far from bright, one cannot fault him in this conclusion. He begins to look extremely angry and the fur on his back stands up in bristles. Somewhat disturbed by Blacky's story and reactions, I made some vague excuse and went off home. But ever since then I've been determined never to catch a rat. However, I did not take up Blacky's invitation to become his associate in prowling after dainties other than rodents. I prefer the cozy life, and it's certainly easier to sleep than to hunt for titbits. Living in a teacher's house, it seems that even a cat acquires the character of teachers. I'd best watch out lest, one of these days, I, too, become dyspeptic.

Talking of teachers reminds me that my master seems recently to have realized his total incapacity as a painter of water-colours; for under the date of December 1st his diary contains the following passage:

At today's gathering I met for the first time a man who shall be nameless. He is said to have led a fast life. Indeed he looks very much a man of the world. Since women like this type of person, it might be more appropriate to say that he has been forced to lead, rather than that he has led, a fast life. I hear his wife was originally a geisha. He is to be envied. For the most part, those who carp at rakes are those incapable of debauchery. Further, many of those who fancy themselves as rakehells are equally incapable of debauchery. Such folk are under no obligation to live fast lives, but do so of their own volition. So I in the matter of water-colors. Neither of us will ever make the grade. And yet this type of debauchee is calmly certain that only he is truly a man of the world. If it is to be accepted that a man can become a man of the world by drinking *saké* in restaurants or by frequenting houses of assignation, then it would seem to follow that I could acquire a name as a painter of water-colors. The notion that my water-color pictures will be better if I don't actually paint them leads me to conclude that a boorish country-bumpkin is in fact far superior to such foolish men of the world.

His observations about men of the world strike me as somewhat unconvincing. In particular his confession of envy in respect of that wife who'd worked as a geisha is positively imbecile and unworthy of a teacher. Nevertheless his assessment of the value of his own water-color painting is certainly just. Indeed my master is a very good judge of his own character but still manages to retain his vanity. Three days later, on December 4th, he wrote in his diary:

Last night I dreamt that someone picked up one of my water-color paintings which I, thinking it worthless, had tossed aside. This person in my dream put the painting in a splendid frame and hung it up on a transom. Staring at my work thus framed, I realized that I have suddenly become a true artist. I feel exceedingly pleased. I spend whole days just staring at my handiwork, happy in the conviction that the picture is a masterpiece. Dawn broke and I woke up: and in the morning sunlight it was obvious that the picture was still as pitiful an object as when I painted it.

The master, even in his dreams, seems burdened with regrets about his water-colors. And men who accept the burdens of regret, whether in respect of water-colors or of anything else, are not the stuff that men of the world are made of.

The day after my master dreamt about the picture, the aesthete in the gold-rimmed spectacles paid a call upon him. He had not visited for some long time. As soon as he was seated he inquired "And how is the painting coming along?"

My master assumed a nonchalant air and answered "Well, I took your advice and I am now busily engaged in sketching. And I must say that when one sketches one seems to apprehend those shapes of things, those delicate changes of color, which hitherto had gone unnoticed. I take it that sketching has developed in the West to its present remarkable condition solely as the result of

the emphasis which, historically, has always
there been placed upon the essentiality
thereof. Precisely as Andrea del Sarto
once observed." Without even so much as
alluding to the passage in his diary, he speaks
approvingly of Andrea del Sarto.

The aesthete scratched his head, and remarked with a laugh "Well actually that
bit about del Sarto was my own invention."

"What was?" My master still fails to
grasp that he's been tricked into making a
fool of himself.

"Why, all that stuff about Andrea del
Sarto whom you so particularly admire. I
made it all up. I never thought you'd take
it seriously." He laughed and laughed,
enraptured with the situation.

I overheard their conversation from my
place on the veranda and I could not help
wondering what sort of entry would appear
in the diary for today. This aesthete is the
sort of man whose sole pleasure lies in
bamboozling people by conversation consist-
ing entirely of humbug. He seems not to
have thought of the effect his twaddle about
Andrea del Sarto must have on my master's
feelings, for he rattled on proudly "Sometimes I cook up a little nonsense and people
take it seriously. Which generates an aesthetic sensation of extreme comicality.
Which I find interesting. The other day, I
told a certain undergraduate that Nicholas
Nickleby had advised Gibbon to cease using
French for the writing of his masterpiece,

The History of French Revolution, and had

indeed persuaded Gibbon to publish it in English. Now this undergraduate was a man of almost eidetic memory, and it was especially amusing to hear him repeating what I told him, word for word and in all seriousness, to a debating session of the Japan Literary Society. And d'you know, there were nearly a hundred in his audience, and all of them sat listening to his drivel with the greatest enthusiasm! In fact, I've another, even better, story. The other day, when I was in the company of some men of letters, one of them happened to mention *Theofano*, Ainsworth's historical novel of the Crusades. I took the occasion to remark that it was a quite outstanding romantic monograph and added the comment that the account of the heroine's death was the epitome of the spectral. The man sitting opposite to me, one who has never uttered the three words 'I don't know', promptly responded that those particular paragraphs were indeed especially fine writing. From which observation I became aware that he, no more than I, had ever read the book."

Wide-eyed, my poor dyspeptic master asked him "Fair enough, but what would you do if the other party had in fact read the book?" It appears that my master is not worried about the dishonesty of the deception, merely about the possible embarrassment of being caught out in a lie. The question leaves the aesthete utterly unfazed.

"Well, if that should happen, I'd say I'd mistaken the title or something like that"; and again, quite unconcerned, he gave himself to laughter.

Though nattily tricked out in gold-rimmed spectacles, his nature is uncommonly akin to that of Rickshaw Blacky. My master said nothing, but blew out smoke-rings as if in confession of his own lack of such audacity. The aesthete (the glitter of whose eyes seemed to be answering "and no wonder; you, being you, could not even cope with water-colors") went on aloud "But, joking apart, painting a picture's a difficult thing. Leonardo da Vinci is supposed once to have told his pupils to make drawings of a stain on the Cathedral wall. The words of a great teacher. In a lavatory for instance, if absorbedly one studies the pattern of the rain-leaks on the wall, a staggering design, a natural creation, invariably emerges. You should keep your eyes open and try drawing from Nature. I'm sure you could make something interesting."

"Is this another of your tricks?"

"No; this one, I promise, is seriously meant. Indeed, I think, don't you, that that image of the lavatory-wall is really rather witty; quite the sort of thing da Vinci would have said."

"Yes, it's certainly witty, " my master somewhat reluctantly conceded. But I do not think he has so far made a drawing in a lavatory.

Rickshaw Blacky has recently gone lame.
His glossy fur has thinned and gradually
grown dull. His eyes, which I once praised
as more beautiful than amber, are now
bleared with mucus. What I notice most is
his loss of all vitality and his sheer physical
deterioration. When last I saw him in the
tea-garden and asked him how he was, the
answer was depressingly precise: "I've had
enough of being farted at by weasels and
crippled with side-swipes from the fishmonger's pole."

The autumn leaves, arranged in two or
three scarlet terraces among the pine-trees,
have fallen like ancient dreams. The red and
white sasanquas near the garden's ornamental
basin, dropping their petals, now a white
and now a red one, are finally left bare. The
wintry sun along the ten-foot length of the
southwards-facing veranda goes down daily
earlier than yesterday. Seldom a day goes
by but a cold wind blows. So my snoozes
have been painfully curtailed.

The master goes to school every day and, as
soon as he returns, shuts himself up in the
study. He tells all visitors that he's tired of
being a teacher. He seldom paints. He's
stopped taking his taka-diastase, saying it
does no good. The children, dear little
things, now trot off, day after day, to kinder-
garten: but on their return, they sing songs,
bounce balls and sometimes hang me up by
the tail.

Since I do not receive any particularly

nourishing food, I have not grown particularly fat; but I struggle on from day to day
keeping myself more or less fit and, so far,
without getting crippled. I catch no rats.
I still detest that O-san. No one has yet
named me but, since it's no use crying for the
moon, I have resolved to remain for the rest
of my life a nameless cat in the house of
this teacher.

S INCE New Year's Day I have acquired a certain modest celebrity: so that, though only a cat, I am feeling quietly proud of myself. Which is not unpleasing.

On the morning of New Year's Day, my master received a picture-postcard, a card of New Year greetings from a certain painter-friend of his. The upper part was painted red, the lower deep green; and right in the center was a crouching animal painted in pastel. The master, sitting in his study, looked at this picture first one way up and then the other. "What fine coloring!" he observed. Having thus expressed his admiration, I thought he had finished with the matter. But no; he continued studying it, first sideways and then longways. In order to examine the object he twists his body, then stretches out his arms like an ancient studying the Book of Divinations and then, turning to face the window, he brings it in to the tip of his nose. I wish he would soon terminate this curious performance, for the action sets his knees a-sway and I find it hard to keep my balance. When at long last the wobbling began to diminish I heard him mutter in a

47

tiny voice "I wonder what it is." Though full of admiration for the colors on the picture-postcard, he couldn't identify the animal painted in its center. Which explained his extraordinary antics. Could it perhaps really be a picture more difficult to interpret than my own first glance had suggested? I half-opened my eyes and looked at the painting with an imperturbable calmness. There could be no shadow of a doubt: it was a portrait of myself. I do not suppose that the painter considered himself an Andrea del Sarto, as did my master; but, being a painter, what he had painted, both in respect of form and of color, was perfectly harmonious. Any fool could see it was a cat. And so skillfully painted that anyone with eyes in his head and the mangiest scrap of discernment would immediately recognize that it was a picture of no other cat but me. To think that anyone should need to go to such painful lengths over such a blatantly simple matter ... I felt a little sorry for the human race. I would have liked to have let him know that the picture is of me. Even if it were too difficult for him to grasp that particularity, I would still have liked to help him see that the painting is a painting of a cat. But since heaven has not seen fit to dower the human animal with an ability to understand cat language, I regret to say that I let the matter be.

Incidentally, I would like to take the occasion of this incident to advise my readers

that the human habit of referring to me in a
scornful tone of voice as some mere trifling
"cat" is an extremely bad one. Humans
appear to think that cows and horses are
constructed from rejected human material,
and that cats are constructed from cow-pats
and horse-dung. Such thoughts, objectively
regarded, are in very poor taste though they
are no doubt not uncommon among teachers
who, ignorant even of their ignorance, remain
self-satisfied with their quaint puffed-up
ideas of their own unreal importance. Even
cats must not be treated roughly or taken for
granted. To the casual observer it may
appear that all cats are the same, facsimiles
in form and substance, as indistinguishable
as peas in a pod; and that no cat can lay claim
to individuality. But once admitted to feline
society, that casual observer would very
quickly realize that things are not so simple,
and that the human saying that "people are
freaks" is equally true in the world of cats.
Our eyes, noses, fur, paws—all of them
differ. From the tilt of one's whiskers to the
set of one's ears, down to the very hang of
one's tail, we cats are sharply differentiated.
In our good looks and our poor looks, in our
likes and dislikes, in our refinement and our
coarsenesses, one may fairly say that cats
occur in infinite variety. Despite the fact
of such obvious differentiation, humans,
their eyes turned up to heaven by reason of
the elevation of their minds or some such
other rubbish, fail to notice even obvious

differences in our external features. That our characters might be characteristic is beyond their comprehension. Which is to be pitied. I understand and endorse the thought behind such sayings as that the cobbler should stick to his last, that birds of a feather flock together, that rice-cakes are for rice-cake makers. For cats, indeed, are for cats. And should you wish to learn about cats, only a cat can tell you. Humans, however advanced, can tell you nothing on this subject. And inasmuch as humans are, in fact, far less advanced than they fancy themselves, they will find it difficult even to start learning about cats. And for an unsympathetic man like my master there's really no hope at all. He does not even understand that love can never grow unless there is at least a complete and mutual understanding. Like an ill-natured oyster, he secretes himself in his study and has never once opened his mouth to the outside world. And to see him there, looking as though he alone has truly attained enlightenment, is enough to make a cat laugh. The proof that he has not attained enlightenment is that, although he has my portrait under his nose, he shows no sign of comprehension but coolly offers such crazy comment as "Perhaps, this being the second year of the war against the Russians, it is a painting of a bear."

As, with my eyes closed, I sat thinking these thoughts on my master's knees, the servant-woman brought in a second picture-postcard. It is a printed picture of a line of

four or five European cats all engaged in
study, holding pens or reading books. One
has broken away from the line to perform a
simple Western dance at the corner of their
common desk. Above this picture "I am a
cat" is written thickly in Japanese black ink.
And down the right-hand side there is even a
haiku stating that "on spring days cats read
books or dance." The card is from one of
the master's old pupils and its meaning should
be obvious to anyone. However my dim-
witted master seems not to understand, for
he looked puzzled and said to himself "Can
this be a Year of the Cat?" He just doesn't
seem to have grasped that these postcards are
manifestations of my growing fame.

At that moment the servant brought in yet
a third postcard. This time the postcard has
no picture; but alongside the characters
wishing my master a happy New Year, the
correspondent has added those for "Please
be so kind as to give my best regards to the
cat." Bone-headed though he is, my master
does appear to get the message when it's
written out thus unequivocally: for he
glanced down at my face and, as if he really
had at last comprehended the situation, said
"hmm." And his glance, unlike his usual
ones, did seem to contain a new modicum of
respect. Which was quite right and proper
considering the fact that it is entirely due to
me that my master, hitherto a nobody, has
suddenly begun to get a name and to attract
attention.

Just then the gate-bell sounded: tinkle-

tinkle, possibly even ting-ting. Probably a visitor. If so, the servant will answer. Since I never go out of my way to investigate callers, except the fishmonger's errand-boy, I remained quietly on my master's knees. The master, however, peered worriedly toward the entrance as if duns were at the door. I deduce that he just doesn't like receiving New Year's callers and sharing a convivial tot. What a marvellous way to be. How much further can pure bigotry go? If he doesn't like visitors, he should have gone out himself; but he lacks even that much enterprise. The inaudacity of his clam-like character grows daily more apparent. A few moments later the servant comes in to say that Mr. Cold-moon has called. I understand that this Coldmoon person was also once a pupil of my master's and that, after leaving school, he so rose in the world as now to be far better-known than his teacher. I don't know why, but this fellow often comes round for a chat. On every such visit he babbles on, with a dreadful sort of coquettishness, about being in love or not in love with somebody or other; about how much he enjoys life or how desperately he is tired of it. And then he leaves. It is quaint enough that to discuss such matters he should seek the company of a withered old nut like my master, but it's quainter still to see my mollusc opening up to comment, now and again, on Coldmoon's mawkish maunderings.

"I'm afraid I haven't been round for quite

some time. Actually I've been as busy as busy since the end of last year and, though I've thought of going out often enough, somehow shanks' pony has just not headed here." Thus, twisting and untwisting the fastening-strings of his short surcoat, Cold-moon babbled on.

"Where then did shanks' pony go?" my master enquired with a serious look as he tugged at the cuffs of his worn black crested surcoat. It is a cotton garment unduly short in the sleeves, and some of its nondescript thin silk lining sticks out about half an inch at the cuffs.

"As it were in various directions," Cold-moon answered; and then laughed. I notice that one of his front teeth is missing.

"What's happened to your teeth?" asks my master, changing the subject.

"Well, actually, at a certain place, I ate mushrooms."

"What did you say you ate?"

"A bit of mushroom. As I tried to bite off a mushroom's umbrella with my front teeth, a tooth just broke off flop."

"Breaking teeth on a mushroom sounds somewhat senile. An image possibly appropriate to a *haiku* but scarcely appropriate to the pursuit of love," remarked my master as he tapped lightly on my head with the palm of his hand.

"Ah! is that *the* cat? But he's quite plump! Sturdy as that, not even Rickshaw Blacky could beat him up. He certainly is a most splendid beast." Coldmoon offers me his homage.

"He's grown quite big lately" responds my master, and proudly smacks me twice upon the head. I am flattered by the compliment but my head feels slightly sore.

"The night before last, what's more, we had a little concert," said Coldmoon going back to his story.

"Where?"

"Surely you don't have to know where. But it was quite interesting; three violins to a piano accompaniment. However unskilled, when there are three of them, violins sound fairly good. Two of them were women and I managed to place myself between them. And I myself, I thought, played rather well."

"Ah, and who were the women?" enviously my master asks. At first glance my master usually looks cold and hard; but, to tell the truth, he is by no means indifferent to women. He once read in a Western novel of a man who invariably fell partially in love with practically every woman that he met. Another character in the book somewhat sarcastically observed that, as a rough calculation, that fellow fell in love with just under seven-tenths of the women he passed in the street. On reading this, my master was struck by its essential truth and remained deeply impressed. Why should a man so impressionable lead such an oysterish existence? A mere cat such as I cannot possibly understand it. Some say it is the result of a love-affair

that went wrong; some say it is due to his
weak stomach; while others simply state that
it's because he lacks both money and audacity. Whatever the truth, it doesn't much
matter since he's a person of insufficient
importance to affect the history of his period.
What is certain is that he did enquire enviously about Coldmoon's female fiddlers. Coldmoon, looking amused, picked up a sliver of
boiled fishpaste in his chopsticks and nipped
at it with his remaining front teeth. I was
worried lest another should fall out. But
this time it was all right.

"Well, both of them are daughters of good
families. You don't know them," Coldmoon coldly answered.

The master drawled "Is—th-a-t—," but
omitted the final "so" which he'd intended.

Coldmoon probably considered it was
about time to be off, for he said "What marvellous weather. If you've nothing better to
do, shall we go out for a walk? As a result
of the fall of Port Arthur," he added encouragingly, "the town's unusually lively."

My master, looking as though he would
sooner discuss the identity of the female
fiddlers than the fall of Port Arthur, hesitated for a moment's thought. But he seemed finally to reach a decision, for he stood up
resolutely and said "All right, let's go out."
He continues to wear his black cotton crested
surcoat and, thereunder, a quilted kimono of
hand-woven silk which, supposedly a keep-
sake of his elder brother, he has worn con-

tinuously for twenty years. Even the most strongly woven silk cannot survive such unremitting, such preternaturally, perennial wear. The material has been worn so thin that, held against the light, one can see the patches sewn on here and there from the inner side. My master wears the same clothes throughout December and January, not bothering to observe the traditional New Year change. He makes, indeed, no distinction between workaday and Sunday clothes. When he leaves the house he saunters out in whatever dress he happens to have on. I do not know whether this is because he has no other clothes to wear or whether, having such clothes, he finds it too much of a bore to change into them. Whatever the case, I can't conceive that these uncouth habits are in any way connected with disappointment in love.

After the two men left, I took the liberty of eating such of the boiled fishpaste as Coldmoon had not already devoured. I am, these days, no longer just a common old cat. I consider myself at least as good as those celebrated in the tales of Momokawa Joen or as that cat of Thomas Gray's which trawled for goldfish. Brawlers such as Rickshaw Blacky are now beneath my notice. I don't suppose anyone will make a fuss if I sneak a bit of fishpaste. Besides, this habit of taking secret snacks between meals is by no means a purely feline custom. O-san, for instance, is always pinching cakes and things which she gobbles

down whenever the mistress leaves the house.
Nor is O-san the only offender: even the
children, of whose refined upbringing the
mistress is continually bragging, display the
selfsame tendency. Only a few days ago
that precious pair woke at some ungodly
hour and, though their parents were still
sound asleep, took it upon themselves to sit
down, face to face, at the dining-table. Now
it is my master's habit every morning to consume most of a loaf of bread, and to give the
children scraps thereof which they eat with a
dusting of sugar. It so happened that on
this day the sugar basin was already on the
table, even a spoon stuck in it. Since there
was no one there to dole them out their
sugar, the elder child scooped up a spoonful
and dumped it on her plate. The younger
followed her elder's fine example and spooned
an equal pile of sugar onto another plate.
For a brief while these charming creatures
just sat and glared at each other. Then the
elder girl scooped a second spoonful onto her
plate, and the younger one proceeded to
equalize the position. The elder sister took
a third spoonful and the younger, in a splendid
spirit of rivalry, followed suit. And so it
went on until both plates were piled high with
sugar and not one single grain remained in
the basin. My master thereupon emerged
from his bedroom rubbing half-sleepy eyes
and proceeded to return the sugar, so labori-
ously extracted by his daughters, back into
the sugar-basin. This incident suggests that,

though egotistical egalitarianism may be more highly developed among humans than among cats, cats are the wiser creatures. My advice to the children would have been to lick the sugar up quickly before it became massed into such senseless pyramids but, because they cannot understand what I say, I merely watched them in silence from my warm morning-place on top of the container for boiled rice.

My master came home late last night from his expedition with Coldmoon. God knows where he went, but it was already past nine before he sat down at the breakfast table. From my same old place I watched his morose consumption of a typical New Year's breakfast of rice-cakes boiled with vegetables, all served up in soup. He takes endless helpings. Though the rice-cakes are admittedly small, he must have eaten some six or seven before, leaving the last one floating in the bowl, "I'll stop now" he remarked and laid his chopsticks down. Should anyone else behave in such a spoilt manner, he could be relied upon to put his foot down: but, vain in the exercise of his petty authority as master of the house, he seems quite unconcerned by the sight of the corpse of a scorched rice-cake drowning in turbid soup. When his wife took taka-diastase from the back of a small cupboard and put it on the table, my master said "I won't take it: it does me no good."

"But they say it's very good after eating

starchy things. I think you should take some." His wife wants him to take it.

"Starchy or not, the stuff's no good." He remains stubborn.

"Really, you are a most capricious man," the mistress mutters as though to herself.

"I'm not capricious: the medicine doesn't work."

"But until the other day you used to say it worked very well and you used to take it every day, didn't you?"

"Yes, it did work until that other day: but it hasn't worked since then": an antithetical answer.

"If you continue in these inconsistencies, taking it one day and stopping it the next, however efficacious the medicine may be, it will never do you any good. Unless you try to be a little more patient, dyspepsia, unlike other illnesses, won't get cured, will it?"; and she turns to O-san who was serving at the table.

"Quite so, madam. Unless one takes it regularly, one cannot find out whether a medicine is a good one or a bad one." O-san readily sides with the mistress.

"I don't care. I don't take it because I don't take it. How can a mere woman understand such things. Keep quiet."

"All right. I'm merely a woman," she says pushing the taka-diastase toward him, quite determined to make him see he is beaten. My master stands up without saying a word and goes off into his study. His wife and servant exchange looks and giggle. If on such occasions I follow him and jump up onto his knees, experience tells me that I shall pay dearly for my folly. Accordingly I go quietly round through the garden and hop up onto the veranda outside his study. I peeped through the slit between the paper sliding-doors and found my master examining a book by somebody called Epictetus. If he could actually understand what he's reading, then he would indeed be worthy of praise. But within five or six minutes he slams the book down on the table. Which is just what I'd suspected. As I sat there watching him, he took out his diary and made the following entry.

"Took a stroll with Coldmoon round Nezu, Ueno, Ikenohata and Kanda. At Ikeno-hata, geishas in formal spring kimono were playing battledore and shuttlecock in front of a house of assignation. Their clothes beautiful: but their faces extremely plain. It occurs to me that they resemble the cat at home."

I don't see why he should single me out as an example of plain features. If I went to a barber and had my face shaved, I wouldn't look much different from a human. But, there you are, humans are conceited and that's the trouble with them.

"As we turned at Hōtan's corner another geisha appeared. She was slim, well-shaped and her shoulders were most beautifully sloped. The way she wore her

mauve kimono gave her a genuine elegance.
"Sorry about last night, Gen-chan—I was
so busy..." She laughed and one
glimpsed white teeth. Her voice was so
harsh, harsh as that of a roving crow, that
her otherwise fine appearance diminished
in enchantment. So much so that I didn't
even bother to turn round to see what sort
of person this Gen-chan was, but saunter-
ed on toward Onarimachi with my hands
tucked inside the breast-fold of my kimono.
Coldmoon, however, seemed to have become a trifle fidgety."

There is nothing more difficult than understanding human mentality. My master's
present mental state is very far from clear; is
he feeling angry or lighthearted, or simply
seeking solace in the scribblings of some dead
philosopher? One just can't tell whether
he's mocking the world or yearning to be
accepted into its frivolous company, whether
he is getting furious over some piddling
little matter or holding himself aloof from
worldly things. Compared with such com-
plexities, cats are truly simple. If we want to
eat, we eat; if we want to sleep, we sleep;
when we are angry, we are angry utterly;
when we cry, we cry with all the desperation
of extreme commitment to our grief. Thus
we never keep things like diaries. For what
would be the point? No doubt human
beings like my two-faced master find it
necessary to keep diaries in order to display
in a darkened room that true character so

assiduously hidden from the world. But among cats both our four main occupations (walking, standing, sitting and lying down) and such incidental activities as excreting waste are pursued quite openly. We live our diaries, and consequently have no need to keep a daily record as a means of maintaining our real characters. Had I the time to keep a diary, I'd use that time to better effect; sleeping on the veranda.

"We dined somewhere in Kanda. Because I allowed myself one or two cups of *saké* (which I had not tasted for quite a time), my stomach this morning feels extremely well. I conclude that the best remedy for a stomach-ailment is *saké* at suppertime. Taka-diastase just won't do. Whatever claims are made for it, it's just no good. That which lacks effect will continue to lack effect."

Thus with his brush he smears the good name of taka-diastase. It is as though he quarrelled with himself, and in this entry one can see a last flash of this morning's ugly mood. Such entries are perhaps most characteristic of human mores.

"The other day, Mr. X claimed that going without one's breakfast helped the stomach. So I took no breakfast for two or three days but the only effect was to make my stomach grumble. Mr. Y strongly advised me to refrain from eating pickles. According to him, all disorders of the stomach originate in pickles. His thesis

was that abstinence from pickles so des-
sicates the sources of all stomach trouble,
that a complete cure must follow. For at
least a week no pickle crossed my lips but,
since that banishment produced no noticeable effect, I have resumed consuming
them. According to Mr. Z, the one true
remedy is ventral massage. But no ordinary massage of the stomach would suffice.
It must be massage in accordance with the
old-world methods of the Minagawa
School. Massaged thus once, or at
most twice, the stomach would be rid of
every ill. The wisest scholars, such as
Yasui Sokuken, and the most resourceful
heroes, such as Sakamoto Ryōma, all relied
upon this treatment. So off I went to
Kaminegishi for an immediate massage.
But the methods used were of inordinate
cruelty. They told me, for instance, that no
good could be hoped for unless one's bones
were massaged; that it would be difficult
properly to eradicate my troubles unless, at
least once, my viscera were totally inverted.
At all events, a single session reduced my
body to the condition of cotton-wool and
I felt as though I had become a lifelong
sufferer from sleeping sickness. I never
went there again. Once was more than
enough. Then Mr. A assured me that one
shouldn't eat solids. So I spent a whole
day drinking nothing but milk. My
bowels gave forth heavy plopping noises as
though they had been swamped, and I

could not sleep all night. Mr. B states that exercising one's intestines by diaphragmic breathing produces a naturally healthy stomach and he counsels me to follow his advice. And I did try. For a time. But it proved no good for it made my bowels queasy. Besides, though every now and again I strive with all my heart and soul to control my breathing with the diaphragm, in five or six minutes I forget to discipline my muscles. And if I concentrate on maintaining that discipline I get so midriff-minded that I can neither read nor write. Waverhouse, my aesthete friend, once found me thus breathing in pursuit a naturally healthy stomach and, rather unkindly, urged me, as a man, to terminate my labor-pangs. So diaphragmic breathing is now also a thing of the past. Dr. C recommends a diet of buckwheat noodles. So buckwheat noodles it was: alternately in soup and served cold after boiling. It did nothing, except loosen my bowels. I have tried every possible means to cure my ancient ailment, but all of them are useless. But those three cups of *saké* which I drank last night with Coldmoon have certainly done some good. From now on, I will drink two or three cups each evening."

I doubt whether this *saké* treatment will be kept up very long. My master's mind exhibits the same incessant changeability as can be seen in the eyes of cats. He has no sense of perseverance. It is, moreover, idiotic that, while he fills his diary with lamentation over his stomach-troubles, he does his best to present a brave face to the world; to grin and bear it. The other day his scholar friend, Professor Whatnot, paid a visit and advanced the theory that it was at least arguable that every illness is the direct result of both ancestral and personal malefaction. He seemed to have studied the matter pretty deeply for the sequence of his logic was clear, consistent and orderly. Altogether it was a fine theory. I am sorry to say that my master has neither the brain nor the erudition to rebut such theories. However, perhaps because he himself was actually suffering from a stomach trouble, he felt obliged to make all sorts of face-saving excuses. He irrelevantly retorted "Your theory is interesting, but are you aware that Carlyle was dyspeptic?" as if claiming that because Carlyle was dyspeptic his own dyspepsia was an intellectual honor. His friend replied "It does not follow that because Carlyle was a dyspeptic, all dyspeptics are Carlyles." My master, reprimanded, held his tongue; but the incident revealed his curious vanity. It's all the more amusing when one recalls that he would probably prefer not to be dyspeptic, for just this morning he recorded in his diary an intention to take treatment by *saké* as from tonight. Now that I've come to think of it, his inordinate consumption of rice-cakes this morning must have been the effect of last night's *saké*-session with Coldmoon. I could have eaten those cakes myself.

Though I am a cat, I eat practically any-

65
·
吾輩は猫である

thing. Unlike Rickshaw Blacky, I lack the energy to go off raiding fishshops up distant alleys. Further, my social status is such that I cannot expect the luxury enjoyed by Tortoiseshell whose mistress teaches the idle rich to play on the two-stringed harp. Therefore I don't, as others can, indulge myself in likes and dislikes. I eat small bits of bread left over by the children, and I lick the jam from bean-jam cakes. Pickles taste awful, but to broaden my experience I once tried a couple of slices of pickled radish. It's a strange thing but, once I've tried it, almost anything turns out edible. To say "I don't like that" or "I don't like this" is mere extravagant willfulness, and a cat that lives in a teacher's house should eschew such fool remarks. According to my master, there was once a novelist whose name was Balzac and he lived in France. He was an extremely extravagant man. I do not mean an extravagant eater but that, being a novelist, he was extravagant in his writing. One day he was trying to find a suitable name for a character in the novel he was writing but, for whatever reason, could not think of a name that pleased him. Just then one of his friends called by, and Balzac suggested they should go out for a walk. This friend had, of course, no idea why; still less that Balzac was determined to find the name he needed. Out on the streets, Balzac did nothing but stare at shop-signboards, but still he couldn't find a suitable name. He marched on endlessly, while his puzzled friend, still ignorant of the object of the expedition, tagged along behind him.

Having fruitlessly explored Paris from morning till evening, they were on their way home when Balzac happened to notice a tailor's signboard bearing the name "Marcus." He clapped his hands. "This is it," he shouted. "It just has to be this. Marcus is a good name, but with a Z in front of Marcus it becomes a perfect name. It has to be a Z. Z. Marcus is remarkably good. Names that I invent are never good. They sound unnatural however cleverly constructed. But now, at long long last, I've got the name I like." Balzac, extremely pleased with himself, was totally oblivious to the inconvenience he had caused his friend. It would seem unduly troublesome that one should have to spend a whole day trudging around Paris merely to find a name for a character in a novel. Extravagance of such enormity acquires a certain splendor but folk like me, a cat kept by a clam-like introvert, cannot even envisage such inordinate behavior. That I should not much care what, so long as it's edible, I eat is probably an inevitable result of my circumstances. Thus it was in no way as an expression of extravagance that I expressed just now my feeling of wishing to eat a rice-cake. I simply thought that I'd better eat while the chance offered, and I then remembered that the piece of rice-cake which my master had left in his breakfast-bowl was possibly still in the kitchen. So round to the kitchen I went.

The rice-cake was stuck, just as I saw it

this morning, at the bottom of the bowl and its color was still as I remembered it. I must confess that I've never previously tasted rice-cake. Yet, though I felt a shade uncertain, it looks quite good to eat. With a tentative front paw I rake at the green vegetables adhering to the rice-cake. My claws, having touched the outer part of the rice-cake, become sticky. I sniff at them and recognize the smell that can be smelt when rice stuck at the bottom of a cooking-pot is transferred into the boiled-rice container. I look around, wondering "Shall I eat it, shall I not?" Fortunately or unfortunately there's nobody about. O-san, with a face that shows no change between year-end and the spring, is playing battledore and shuttlecock. The children in the inner room are singing something about a rabbit and a tortoise. If I am to eat this New Year speciality, now's the moment. If I miss this chance I shall have to spend a whole long year not knowing how a rice-cake tastes. At this point, though a mere cat, I perceived a truth: that golden opportunity makes all animals venture to do even those things they do not want to do. To tell the truth, I do not particularly want to eat the rice-cake. In fact the more I examined the thing at the bottom of the bowl the more nervous I became and the more keenly disinclined to eat it. If only O-san would open the kitchen door or if I could hear the children's footsteps coming toward me, I would unhesitatingly abandon the bowl: nor only that, I would have put away all thought of rice-cakes for another year. But no one comes. I've hesitated long enough. Still no one comes. I feel as if someone were hotly urging me on, someone whispering "Eat it, quickly!" I looked into the bowl and prayed that someone would appear. But no one did. I shall have to eat the rice-cake after all. In the end, lowering the entire weight of my body into the bottom of the bowl, I bit about an inch deep into a corner of the rice-cake.

Most things that I bite that hard come clean off in my mouth. But what a surprise! For I found when I tried to reopen my jaw that it would not budge. I try once again to bite my way free, but find I'm stuck. Too late I realize that the rice-cake is a fiend. When a man who has fallen into a marsh struggles to escape, the more he thrashes about trying to extract his legs the deeper in he sinks. Just so, the harder I clamp my jaws the more my mouth grows heavy and my teeth immobilized. I can feel the resistance to my teeth; but that's all. I cannot dispose of it. Waverhouse, the aesthete, once described my master as an aliquant man and I must say it's rather a good description. This rice-cake too, like my master, is aliquant. It looked to me that, however much I continued biting, nothing could ever result: the process could go on and on eternally like the division of ten by three. In the middle of this anguish I found my second truth: that all animals can tell by instinct what is or is not good for them. Although I have now discovered two great truths, I remain unhappy by reason of the adherent rice-cake. My teeth are being sucked into its body, and are becoming excruciatingly painful. Unless I can complete my bite and run away quickly, O-san will be on me. The children seem to have stopped singing, and I'm sure they'll soon come running into the kitchen. In an extremity of anguish, I lashed about with my tail; but to no effect. I made my ears stand up and then lie flat, but this didn't help either. Come to think of it, my ears and tail have nothing to do with the rice-cake. In short, I had indulged in a waste of wagging, a waste of ear-erection and a waste of flattening ears. So I stopped.

At long last it dawned on me that the best thing to do is to force the rice-cake down by using my two front paws. First I raised my right paw and stroked it round my mouth. Naturally this mere stroking brought no relief whatever. Next, I stretched out my left paw and with it scraped quick circles round my mouth. These ineffectual passes failed to exorcize the fiend in the rice-cake. Realizing that it was essential to proceed with patience, I scraped alternatively with my right and left paws, but my teeth stayed stuck in the rice-cake. Growing impatient, I now used both front paws simultaneously. Then, only then, I found to my amazement that I could actually stand up on my hind legs. Somehow I feel un-catlike. But not caring

whether I am a cat or not, I scratch away like
mad at my whole face in frenzied determination to keep on scratching until the fiend in
the rice-cake has been driven out. Since the
movements of my front paws are so vigorous
I am in danger of losing my balance and falling down. To keep my equilibrium I find
myself marking time with my hind legs. I
begin to tittup from one spot to another, and
I finish up prancing madly all over the kitch-
en. It gives me great pride to realize that I
can so dextrously maintain an upright position, and the revelation of a third great truth
is thus vouchsafed me: that in conditions of
exceptional danger one can surpass one's
normal level of achievement. This is the
real meaning of Special Providence.

Sustained by Special Providence, I am
fighting for dear life against that demonic rice-
cake when I hear footsteps. Someone seems
to be approaching. Thinking it would be
fatal to be caught in this predicament, I re-
double my efforts and am positively running
around the kitchen. The footsteps come
closer and closer. Alas, that Special Providence seems not to last for ever. In the end
I am discovered by the children who loudly
shout "Why look! The cat's been eating
rice-cakes and is dancing." The first to hear
their announcement was that O-san person.
Abandoning her shuttlecock and battledore,
she flew in through the kitchen-door crying
"Gracious me!" Then the mistress, sedate
in her formal silk kimono, deigns to remark

"What a naughty cat." And my master, drawn from his study by the general hubbub, shouts "You fool!" The children find me funniest, but by general agreement the whole household is having a good old laugh. It is annoying: it is painful: it is impossible to stop dancing. Hell and damnation! When at long last the laughter began to die down, the dear little five-year-old piped up with an "Oh what a comical cat," which had the effect of renewing the tide of their ebbing laughter. They fairly split their sides. I have already heard and seen quite a lot of heartless human behavior, but never before have I felt so bitterly critical of their conduct. Special Providence having vanished into thin air, I was back in my customary position on all fours, finally at my wit's end and, by reason of giddiness, cutting a quite ridiculous figure. My master seems to have felt it would be perhaps a pity to let me die before his very eyes, for he said to O-san "Help him get rid of that rice-cake." O-san looks at the mistress as if to say "Why not make him go on dancing?" The mistress would gladly see my minuet continued but, since she would not go so far as wanting me to dance myself to death, says nothing. My master turned somewhat sharply to the servant and ordered "Hurry it up: if you don't help quickly the cat will be dead." O-san, with a vacant look on her face as though she had been roughly wakened from some peculiarly delicious dream, took a firm grip on the rice-cake and

yanked it out of my mouth. I am not quite
as feeble-fanged as Coldmoon but I really
did think my entire front toothwork was
about to break off. The pain was inde-
scribable. The teeth embedded in the rice-
cake are being pitilessly wrenched. You
can't imagine what it was like. It was then
that the fourth enlightenment burst upon me:
that all comfort is achieved through hardship.
When at last I came to myself and looked
around at a world restored to normality, all
the members of the household had disappeared into the inner room.

Having made such a fool of myself, I feel
quite unable to face such hostile critics as
O-san. It would, I think, unhinge my mind.
To restore my mental tranquillity, I decided to
visit Tortoiseshell so I left the kitchen and set
off through the backyard to the house of the
two-stringed harp. Tortoiseshell is a celebrated beauty in our district. Though I am
undoubtedly a cat, I possess a wide general
knowledge of the nature of compassion and
am deeply sensitive to affection, kind-hearted-
ness, tenderness and love. Merely to observe
the bitterness in my master's face, just to be
snubbed by O-san, leaves me out of sorts.
At such times I visit this fair lady friend of
mine and our conversation ranges over many
things. Then, before I am aware of it, I find
myself refreshed. I forget my worries, hardships, everything. I feel as if reborn.
Female influence is indeed a most potent
thing. Through a gap in the cedar-hedge, I

peer to see if she is anywhere about. Tortoiseshell, wearing a smart new collar in celebration of the season, is sitting very neatly on her veranda. The rondure of her back is indescribably beautiful. It is the most beautiful of all curved lines. The way her tail curves, the way she folds her legs, the charmingly lazy shake of her ears—all these are quite beyond description. She looks so warm sitting there so gracefully in the very sunniest spot. Her body holds an attitude of utter stillness and correctness. And her fur, glossy as velvet that reflects the rays of spring, seems suddenly to quiver although the air is still. For a while I stood, completely enraptured, gazing at her. Then as I came to myself, I softly called "Miss Tortoiseshell, Miss Tortoiseshell" and beckoned with my paw.

"Why, Professor", she greeted me as she stepped down from the veranda. A tiny bell attached to her scarlet collar made little tinkling sounds. I say to myself "Ah, it's for the New Year that she's wearing a bell" and, while I am still admiring its lively tinkle, find she has arrived beside me. "A happy New Year, Professor," and she waves her tail to the left; for when cats exchange greetings one first holds one's tail upright like a pole, then twists it round to the left. In our neighborhood it is only Tortoiseshell who calls me Professor. Now I have already mentioned that I have as yet no name; but it is Tortoiseshell, and she alone, who pays me

house. Indeed, I am not altogether displeased to be addressed as a Professor, and
respond willingly to her apostrophe.

"And a happy New Year to you," I say.
"How beautifully you're got up!"

"Yes, the mistress bought it for me at the
end of last year. Isn't it nice?" and she
makes it tinkle for me.

"Yes indeed, it has a lovely sound. I've
never seen such a wonderful thing in my life."

"No! Everyone's using them," and she
tinkle-tinkles. "But isn't it a lovely sound?
I'm so happy." She tinkle-tinkle-tinkles
continuously.

"I can see your mistress loves you very
dearly." Comparing my lot with hers, I
hinted at my envy of a pampered life.

Tortoiseshell is a simple creature. "Yes,"
she says, "that's true; she treats me as if I
were her own child." And she laughs innocently. It is not true that cats never laugh.
Human beings are mistaken in their belief
that only they are capable of laughter. When
I laugh my nostrils grow triangular and my
Adam's apple trembles. No wonder human
beings fail to understand it.

"What really is your master like?"

"My master? That sounds strange. Mine
is a mistress. A mistress of the two-stringed
harp."

"I know that. But what is her background? I imagine she's a person of high
birth?"

"Ah, yes."

> *A small Princess-pine*
> *While waiting for you . . .*

Beyond the sliding paper-door the mistress begins to play on her two-stringed harp.

"Isn't that a splendid voice?" Tortoise-shell is proud of it.

"It seems extremely good, but I don't understand what she's singing. What's the name of the piece?"

"That? Oh, it's called something or other. The mistress is especially fond of it. D'you know, she's actually sixty-two. But in excellent condition, don't you think?"

I suppose one has to admit that she's in excellent condition if she's still alive at sixty-two. So I answered "Y-es." I thought to myself that I'd given a silly answer, but I could do no other since I couldn't think of anything brighter to say.

"You may not think so, but she used to be a person of high standing. Always she tells me so."

"What was she originally?"

"I understand that she's the thirteenth Shogun's widowed wife's private-secretary's younger sister's husband's mother's nephew's daughter."

"What?"

"The thirteenth Shogun's widowed wife's private-secretary's younger sister's . . ."

"Ah! But, please, not quite so fast. The thirteenth Shogun's widowed wife's younger sister's private-secretary's . . ."

widowed wife's private secretary's younger
sister's . . ."

"The thirteenth Shogun's widowed
wife's . . ."

"Right."

"Private-secretary's. Right?"

"Right."

"Husband's . . ."

"No, younger sister's husband's."

"Of course. How could I? Younger
sister's husband's . . ."

"Mother's nephew's daughter. There you
are."

"Mother's nephew's daughter?"

"Yes, you've got it."

"Not really. It's so terribly involved that
I still can't get the hang of it. What exactly
is her relation to the thirteenth Shogun's
widowed wife?"

"Oh, but you are so stupid! I've just been
telling you what she is. She's the thirteenth
Shogun's widowed wife's private-secretary's
younger sister's husband's mother's . . ."

"That much I've followed, but . . ."

"Then, you've got it: haven't you?"

"Yes." I had to give in. There are times
and times for little white lies.

Beyond the sliding paper-door the sound of
the two-stringed harp came to a sudden stop
and the mistress' voice called "Tortoiseshell,
Tortoiseshell, your lunch is ready." Tortoiseshell looked happy and remarked "There,
she's calling, so I must go home. I hope

you'll forgive me?" What would be the good of my saying that I mind? "Come and see me again," she said; and she ran off through the garden tinkling her bell. But suddenly she turned and came back to ask me anxiously "You're looking far from well. Is anything wrong?" I couldn't very well tell her that I'd eaten a rice-cake and gone dancing; so "No," I said, "nothing in particular. I did some weighty thinking which brought on something of a headache. Indeed I called today because I fancied that just to talk with you would help me to feel better."

"Really? Well, take good care of yourself. Good-bye now." She seemed a tiny bit sorry to leave me, which has completely restored me to the liveliness I'd felt before the rice-cake bit me. I now felt wonderful and decided to go home through that tea-plantation where one could have the pleasure of treading down lumps of half-melted frost. I put my face through the broken bamboo hedge, and there was Rickshaw Blacky, back again on the dry chrysanthemums, yawning his spine into a high black arch. Nowadays I'm no longer scared of Blacky but, since any conversation with him involves the risk of trouble, I endeavor to pass, cutting him dead. But it's not in Blacky's nature to contain his feelings if he believes himself looked down upon. "Hey you, Mr. No-name. You're very stuck-up these days, now aren't you? You may be living in a teacher's house, but don't go giving yourself such airs.

And stop, I warn you, trying to make a fool of me." Blacky doesn't seem to know that I am now a celebrity. I wish I could explain the situation to him but, since he's not the kind who can understand such things, I decide simply to offer him the briefest of greetings and then to take my leave as soon as I decently can.

"A happy New Year, Mr. Blacky. You do look well. As usual." And I lift up my tail and twist it to the left. Blacky, keeping his tail straight up, refused to return my salutation.

"What! Happy? If the New Year's happy, then you should be out of your tiny mind the whole year round. Now push off sharp, you back-end of a bellows."

That turn of phrase about the back-end of a bellows sounds distinctly derogatory, but its semantic content happened to escape me. "What," I enquired, "do you mean by the back-end of a bellows?"

"You're being sworn at and you stand there asking its meaning. I give up! I really do! You really are a New Year's nit."

A New Year's nit sounds somewhat poetic, but its meaning is even more obscure than that bit about the bellows. I would have liked to ask the meaning for my future reference but, as it was obvious I'd get no clear answer, I just stood facing him without a word. I was actually feeling rather awkward, but just then the wife of Blacky's master suddenly screamed out "Where in hell's that cut of salmon I left here on the shelf? My God, I do declare that hellcat's been and snitched it once again! That's the nastiest cat I've ever seen. See what he'll get when he comes back!" Her raucous voice unceremoniously shakes the mild air of the season, vulgarizing its natural peacefulness. Blacky puts on an impudent look as if to say "If you want to scream your head off, scream away"; and he jerked his square chin forward at me as if to say "Did you hear that hullaballoo?" Up to this point I've been too busy talking to Blacky to notice or think about anything else; but now, glancing down, I see between his legs a mud-covered bone from the cheapest cut of salmon.

"So you've been at it again!" Forgetting our recent exchanges, I offered Blacky my usual flattering exclamation. But it was not enough to restore him to good humor.

"Been at it! What the hell d'you mean, you saucy blockhead? And what do you mean by saying 'again' when this is nothing but a skinny slice of the cheapest fish? Don't you know who I am! I'm Rickshaw Blacky, damn you." And, having no shirt-sleeves to roll up, he lifts an aggressive right front-paw as high as his shoulder.

"I've always known you were Mr. Rickshaw Blacky."

"If you knew, why the hell did you say I'd been at it again? Answer me!" And he blows out over me great gusts of oven breath. Were we human beings, I would be being

shaken by the collar of my coat. I am somewhat taken aback and am indeed wondering
how possibly to get out of the situation, when
that woman's fearful voice is heard again.

"Hey! Mr. Westbrook. You there, Westbrook, can you hear me? Listen, I got
something to say. Bring me a pound of beef.
And quick. O.K.? Understand? Beef that
isn't tough. A pound of it. See?" Her
beef-demanding tones shatter the peace of the
whole neighborhood.

"It's only once a year she orders beef and
that's why she shouts so loud. She wants
the entire neighborhood to know about her
marvellous pound of beef. What can one do
with a woman like that!" asked Blacky
jeeringly as he stretched all four of his legs.
As I can find nothing to say in reply, I keep
silent and watch.

"A miserable pound just simply will not do.
But I reckon it can't be helped. Hang on to
that beef. I'll have it later." Blacky com-
munes with himself as though the beef had
been ordered specially for him.

"This time you're in for a real treat.
That's wonderful!" With these words I'd
hoped to pack him off to his home.

But Blacky snarled "That's nothing to do
with you. Just shut your big mouth, you!";
and using his strong hind-legs, he suddenly
scrabbles up a torrent of fallen icicles which
thuds down on my head. I was taken completely aback and, while I was still busy
shaking the muddy debris off my body,

Blacky slid off through the hedge and disappeared. Presumably to possess himself of Westbrook's beef.

When I get home I find the place unusually spring-like and even the master is laughing gaily. Wondering why, I hopped onto the veranda and, as I padded to sit beside the master, noticed an unfamiliar guest. His hair is parted neatly and he wears a crested cotton surcoat and a duckcloth *hakama*. He looks like a student and, at that, an extremely serious one. Lying on the corner of my master's small hand-warming brazier, right beside the lacquer cigarette-box, there's a visiting card on which is written "To introduce Mr. Beauchamp Blowlamp: from Coldmoon." Which tells me both the name of this guest and the fact that he's a friend of Coldmoon. The conversation going on between host and guest sounds enigmatic because I missed the start of it. But I gather that it has something to do with Waverhouse, the aesthete whom I have had previous occasion to mention.

"And he urged me to come along with him because it would involve an ingenious idea, he said." The guest is talking calmly.

"Do you mean there was some ingenious idea involved in lunching at a Western style restaurant?" My master pours more tea for the guest and pushes the cup toward him.

"Well, at the time I did not understand what this ingenious idea could be; but, since it was *his* idea, I thought it bound to be something interesting and . . ."

"So you accompanied him.   I see."

"Yes, but I got a surprise."

The master, looking as if to say "I told you so," gives me a whack on the head.   Which hurts a little.   "I expect it proved somewhat farcical.   He's rather that way inclined." Clearly, he has suddenly remembered that business with Andrea del Sarto.

"Ah yes?   Well, as he suggested we would be eating something special . . ."

"What did you have?"

"First of all, while studying the menu, he gave me all sorts of information about food."

"Before ordering any?"

"Yes."

"And then?"

"And then, turning to a waiter, he said 'There doesn't seem to be anything special on the card.'   The waiter, not to be outdone, suggested roast duck or veal chops.   Whereupon Waverhouse remarked quite sharply that we hadn't come a very considerable distance just for common or garden fare.   The waiter, who didn't understand the significance of common or garden, looked puzzled and said nothing."

"So I would imagine."

"Then, turning to me, Waverhouse observed that in France or in England one can obtain any amount of dishes cooked *à la Tenmei* or *à la Manyō* but that in Japan, wherever you go, the food is all so stereotyped that one doesn't even feel tempted to enter a restaurant of the so-called Western style.   And so on and so on.   He was in tremendous form. But has he ever been abroad?"

"Waverhouse abroad? Of course not. He's got the money and the time. If he wanted to, he could go off anytime. Probably he just converted his future intention to travel into the past tense of widely traveled experience as a sort of joke." The master flatters himself that he has said something witty and laughs invitingly. His guest looks largely unimpressed.

"I see. I wondered when he'd been abroad. I took everything he said quite seriously. Besides, he described such things as snail-soup and stewed frogs as though he'd really seen them with his own two eyes."

"He must have heard about them from someone. He's an adept at such terminological inexactitudes."

"So it would seem," and Beauchamp stares down at the narcissus in a vase. He seems a little disappointed.

"So that then was his ingenious idea, I take it?" asks the master still in quest of certainties.

"No, that was only the beginning. The main part's still to come."

"Ah!" The master utters an interjection mingled with curiosity.

"Having finished his dissertation on matters gastronomical and European, he proposed 'since it's quite impossible to obtain snails or frogs, however much we may desire them, let's at least have moat-bells: what do you say?" And without really giving the matter any thought at all, I answered 'Yes, that would be fine'."

"Moat-bells sound a little odd."

"Yes, very odd: but because Waverhouse was speaking so seriously, I didn't then notice the oddity." He seems to be apologizing to my master for his carelessness.

"What happened next?" asks my master quite indifferently and without any sign of sympathetic response to his guest's implied apology.

"Well, then he told the waiter to bring moat-bells for two. The waiter said 'Do you mean meat-balls, sir?' but Waverhouse, assuming an ever more serious expression, corrected him with gravity. 'No, not meat-balls: moat-bells'."

"Really? But is there any such dish as moat-bells?"

"Well I thought it sounded somewhat strange; but as Waverhouse was so calmly sure and is so great an authority on all things Occidental—remember it was then my firm belief that he was widely traveled—I too joined in and explained to the waiter 'Moat-bells, my good man; moat-bells'."

"What did the waiter do?"

"The waiter—it's really rather funny now one comes to think back on it—looked thoughtful for a while and then said 'I'm terribly sorry sir, but today unfortunately we have no moat-bells. Though should you care for meat-balls we could serve you, sir,

immediately.' Waverhouse thereupon looked extremely put out and said, 'So, we've
come all this long way for nothing. Couldn't
you really manage moat-bells? Please do
see what can be done'; and he slipped a small
tip to the waiter. The waiter said he would
ask the cook again and went off into the
kitchen."

"He must have had his mind dead set on
eating moat-bells."

"After a brief interval the waiter returned
to say that if moat-bells were ordered specially they could be provided, but that it would
take a long time. Waverhouse was quite
composed. He said 'It's the New Year and
we are in no kind of hurry. So let's wait for
it?' He drew a cigar from the inside of his
Western suit and lighted up in the most
leisurely manner. I felt called upon to match
his cool composure so, taking the *Japan
News* from my kimono-pocket, I started
reading it. The waiter retired for further
consultations."

"What a business!" My master leans
forward, showing quite as much enthusiasm
as he does when reading war news in the
dailies.

"The waiter re-emerged with apologies
and the confession that, of late, the ingredients of moat-bells were in such short supply
that one could not get them at Kameya's nor
even down at No. 15 in Yokohama. He
expressed regret, but it seemed certain that
the material for moat-bells would not be

back in stock for some considerable time.
Waverhouse then turned to me and repeated,
over and over again, 'What a pity: and we
came especially for that dish.' I felt that I
had to say something, so I joined him in
saying 'Yes, it's a terrible shame! Really, a
great great pity!'"

"Quite so" agrees my master, though I
myself don't follow his reasoning.

"These observations must have made the
waiter feel quite sorry, for he said 'When, one
of these days, we do have the necessary ingredients, we'd be happy if you would come,
sir, and sample our fare.' But when Waverhouse proceeded to ask him what ingredients
the restaurant did use, the waiter just laughed
and gave no answer. Waverhouse then pres-
singly enquired if the key-ingredient happened to be Tochian (who, as you know, is a
haiku poet of the Nihon School); and d'you
know, the waiter answered 'Yes, it is, sir; and
that is precisely why none is currently available even in Yokohama. I am indeed' he
added, 'most regretful, sir'."

"Ha-ha-ha! So that's the point of the
story? How very funny!" and the master,
quite unlike his usual self, roars with laughter.
His knees shake so much that I nearly tumble
off. Paying no regard to my predicament,
the master laughs and laughs. He seems
suddenly deeply pleased to realize that he is
not alone in being gulled by Andrea del
Sarto.

"And then, as soon as we were out in the

street, he said 'You see, we've done well. That ploy about the moat-bells was really rather good, wasn't it?'; and he looked as pleased as Punch. I let it be known that I was lost in admiration, and so we parted. However, since by then it was well past the lunch-hour, I was nearly starving."

"That must have been very trying for you." My master shows, for the first time, a sympathy to which I have no objection. For a while there was a pause in the conversation and my purring could be heard by host and guest.

Mr. Beauchamp drains his cup of tea, now quite cold, in one quick gulp and with some formality remarks "As a matter of fact I've come today to ask a favor from you."

"Yes? And what can I do for you?" My master, too, assumes a formal face.

"As you know, I am a devotee of literature and art . . ."

"That's a good thing," replies my master quite encouragingly.

"Since a little while back, I and a few like-minded friends have got together and organized a reading-group. The idea is to meet once a month for the purpose of continued studying in this field. In fact, we've already had the first meeting—at the end of last year."

"May I ask you a question? When you say, like that, a reading-group, it suggests that you engage in reading poetry and prose in a singsong tone. But in what sort of manner do you, in fact, proceed?"

"Well, we are beginning with ancient works but we intend to consider the works of our fellow-members."

"When you speak of ancient works, do you mean something like Po Chü-i's *Lute Song*?"

"No."

"Perhaps things like Buson's mixture of *haiku* and Chinese verse?"

"No."

"What kinds of thing do you then do?"

"The other day, we did one of Chikamatsu's lovers' suicides."

"Chikamatsu? You mean the Chikamatsu who wrote *jōruri* plays?" There are not two Chikamatsus. When one says Chikamatsu, one does indeed mean Chikamatsu the playwright and could mean nobody else. I thought my master really stupid to ask so fool a question. However, oblivious to my natural reactions, he gently strokes my head. I calmly let him go on stroking me, justifying my compliance with the reflection that so small a weakness is permissible when there are those in the world who admit to thinking themselves under loving observation by persons who merely happen to be cross-eyed.

Beauchamp answers "Yes," and tries to read the reaction on my master's face.

"Then is it one person who reads or do you allot parts among you?"

"We allot parts and each reads out the appropriate dialogue. The idea is to empathize with the characters in the play and, above all, to bring out their individual personalities. We do gestures as well. The main thing is to catch the essential character of the era of the play. Accordingly the lines are read out as if spoken by each character, which may perhaps be a young lady or possibly an errand-boy."

"In that case it must be like a play."

"Yes; almost the only things missing are the costumes and the scenery."

"May I ask if your reading was a success?"

"For a first attempt, I think one might claim that it was, if anything, a success."

"And which lovers' suicide play did you perform on the last occasion?"

"We did a scene in which a boatman takes a fare to the red light quarter of Yoshiwara."

"You certainly picked on a most irregular incident, didn't you?" My master, being a teacher, tilts his head a little sideways as if regarding something slightly doubtful. The cigarette-smoke drifting from his nose passes up by his ear and along the side of his head.

"No, it isn't that irregular. The characters are a passenger, a boatman, a high-class prostitute, a serving-girl, an ancient crone of a brothel-attendant and, of course, a geisha-registrar. But that's all." Beauchamp seems utterly unperturbed. My master, on hearing the words "a high-class prostitute," winces slightly but probably only because he's not well up in the meanings of such technical terms as *nakai*, *yarite* and *kemban*. He seeks to clear the ground with a question. "Does not *nakai* signify something like a maid-servant in a brothel?"

"Though I have not yet given the matter my full attention, I believe that *nakai* signifies a serving-girl in a teahouse and that *yarite* is some sort of an assistant in the women's quarters." Although Beauchamp recently claimed that his group seeks to impersonate the actual voices of the characters in the plays, he does not seem to have fully grasped the real nature of *yarite* and *nakai*.

"I see, *nakai* belong to a teahouse while *yarite* live in a brothel. Next, are *kemban* human beings or is it the name of a place? If human, are they men or women?"

"*Kemban*, I rather think, is a male human being."

"What is his function?"

"I've not yet studied that far. But I'll make inquiries, one of these days."

Thinking, in the light of these revelations, that the play-readings must be affairs extraordinarily ill-conducted, I glance up at my master's face. Surprisingly, I find him looking serious. "Apart from yourself, who were the other readers taking part?"

"A wide variety of people. Mr. K, a Bachelor of Law, played the high-class prostitute, but his delivery of that woman's sugary dialogue through his very male mustache did, I confess, create a slightly queer impression. And then there was a scene in which this *oiran* was seized with spasms . . ."

"Do your readers extend their reading

activities to the simulation of spasms?" asked my master anxiously.

"Yes indeed; for expression is, after all, important." Beauchamp clearly considers himself a literary artist *à l'outrance*.

"Did he manage to have his spasms nicely?" My master has made a witty remark.

"The spasms were perhaps the only thing beyond our capability at such a first endeavor." Beauchamp, too, is capable of wit.

"By the way," asks my master, "What part did you take?"

"I was the boatman."

"Really? You, the boatman!" My master's tone was such as to suggest that, if Beauchamp could be a boatman, he himself could be a geisha-registrar. Switching his tone to one of simple candor, he then asks: "Was the role of the boatman too much for you?"

Beauchamp does not seem particularly offended. Maintaining the same calm voice, he replies "As a matter of fact, it was because of this boatman that our precious gathering, though it went up like a rocket, came down like a stick. It so happened that four or five girl-students are living in the boarding-house next door to our meeting-hall. I don't know how, but they found out when our reading was to take place. Anyway it appears that they came and listened to us under the window of the hall. I was doing the boatman's voice and, just when I had

warmed up nicely and was really getting into
the swing of it—perhaps my gestures were a
a little over-exaggerated—anyway the girl
students, all of whom had managed to control
their feelings up to that point, thereupon burst
out into simultaneous cachinnations. I was
of course surprised, and I was of course
embarrassed: indeed, thus dampened, I
could not find it in me to continue. So our
meeting came to an end." If this were considered a success, even for a first meeting,
what would failure have been like? I could
not help laughing. Involuntarily, my
Adam's apple made a rumbling noise. My
master, who likes what he takes to be purring,
strokes my head ever more and more gently.
I'm thankful to be loved just because I laugh
at someone, but at the same time I feel a bit
uneasy.

"What very bad luck!" My master offers
condolences despite the fact that we are still
in the congratulatory season of the New Year.

"As from our second, that is our next,
meeting we intend to make a great advance
and manage things in the grand style. That,
in fact, is the very reason for my call today:
we'd like you to join our group and help us."

"I can't possibly have spasms." My
negative-minded master is already poised to
refuse.

"No, you don't have to have spasms or
anything like that. Here's a list of the
patron-members." So saying, Beauchamp
very carefully produced a small notebook

from a purple-col   carrying-wrapper. He opened the notebc k and placed it in front of my master's knees. "Will you please sign and make your seal-mark here?" I see that the book contains the names of distinguished Doctors of Literature and Bachelors of Arts of this present day, all neatly mustered in full force.

"Well, I wouldn't say I object to becoming a supporter; but what sort of obligations would I have to meet?" My oyster-like master displays his apprehensions . . .

"There's hardly any obligation. We ask nothing from you except a signature expressing your approval."

"Well, in that case, I'll join." As he realizes that there is no real obligation involved, he suddenly becomes lighthearted. His face assumes the expression of one who would sign even a secret commitment to engage in rebellion provided it was clear that the signature carried no binding obligation. Besides, it is understandable that he should assent so eagerly: for to be included, even by name only, among so many names of celebrated scholars is a supreme honor for one who has never before had such an opportunity. "Excuse me," and my master goes off to the study to fetch his seal. I am tipped to fall unceremoniously onto the matting. Beauchamp helps himself to a slice of sponge-cake from the cake-bowl and crams it into his mouth. For a while he seems to be in pain, mumbling. Just for a second ι

am reminded of my morning experience with
the rice-cake. My master reappears with his
seal just as the sponge-cake settles down in
Beauchamp's bowels. My master does not
seem to notice that a piece of sponge-cake is
missing from the cake-bowl. If he does, I
shall be the first to be suspected.

Mr. Beauchamp having taken his depar-
ture, my master reenters the study where he
finds on his desk a letter from friend Waverhouse.

"I wish you a Very Happy New Year . . ."

My master considers the letter to have
started with an unusual seriousness. Letters
from Waverhouse are seldom serious. The
other day, for instance, he wrote: "Of late,
as I am not in love with any woman, I receive
no love letters from anywhere. As I am more
or less alive, please set your mind at ease."
Compared with which, this New Year's letter
is exceptionally matter-of-fact:

"I would like to come and see you; but I
am so very extremely busy every day because, contrary to your negativism, I am
planning to greet this New Year, a year
unprecedented in all history, with as
positive an attitude as is possible. Hoping
you will understand . . ."

My master quite understands, thinking that
Waverhouse, being Waverhouse, must be
busy having fun during the New Year season.

"Yesterday, finding a minute to spare, I
sought to treat Mr. Beauchamp to a dish of
moat-bells: unfortunately, due to a short-

age of their ingredients, I could not carry out my intention. It was most regrettable. . ."

My master smiles, thinking that the letter is falling more into the usual pattern.

"Tomorrow there will be a card-party at a certain Baron's house; the day after tomorrow a New Year's banquet at the Society of Aesthetes; and the day after that, a welcoming party for Professor Toribe; and on the day thereafter . . ."

My master, finding it rather a bore, skips a few lines.

"So you see, because of these incessant parties—nō-song parties, *haiku* parties, *tanka* parties, parties even for New Style Poetry, and so on and so on, I am perpetually occupied for quite some time. And that is why I am obliged to send you this New Year's letter instead of calling on you in person. I pray you will forgive me . . ."

"Of course you do not have to call on me." My master voices his answer to the letter.

"Next time that you are kind enough to visit me, I would like you to stay and dine. Though there is no special delicacy in my poor larder, at least I hope to be able to offer you some moat-bells and I am indeed looking forward to that pleasure . . ."

"He's still brandishing his moat-bells," muttered my master who, thinking the invitation an insult, begins to feel indignant.

"However, because the ingredients neces-

currently in rather short supply, it may not
be possible to arrange it. In which case,
I will offer you some peacocks' tongues . . ."

"Aha! so he's got two strings to his bow,"
thinks my master and cannot resist reading
the rest of the letter.

"As you know, the tongue-meat per peacock amounts to less than half the bulk of
the small finger. Therefore, in order to
satisfy your gluttonous stomach . . ."

"What a pack of lies" remarks my master
in a tone of resignation.

"I think one needs to catch at least twenty
or thirty peacocks. However, though one
sees an occasional peacock, maybe two, at
the zoo or at the Asakusa Amusement
Center, there are none to be found at my
poulterer's: which is occasioning me pain,
great pain . . ."

"You're having that pain of your own free
will." My master shows no evidence of
gratitude.

"The dish of peacocks' tongues was once
extremely fashionable in Rome when the
Roman Empire was in the full pride of its
prosperity. How I have always secretly
coveted after peacocks' tongues, that acme
of gastronomical luxury and elegance, you
may well imagine . . ."

"I may well imagine, may I? How ridiculous." My master is extremely cold.

"From that time forward until about the
sixteenth century, peacock was an indis-

pensable delicacy at all banquets. If my memory serves me, when the Earl of Leicester invited Queen Elizabeth to Kenilworth, peacocks' tongues were on the menu. And in one of Rembrandt's banquet-scenes a peacock is clearly to be seen, lying in its pride upon the table . . ."

My master grumbles that if Waverhouse can find time to compose a history of the eating of peacocks, he cannot be really so busy.

"Anyway if I go on eating good food as I have been doing recently, I will doubtless end up one of these days with a stomach weak as yours . . ."

" 'Like yours' is quite unecessary. He has no need to establish me as the prototypical dyspeptic," grumbles my master.

"According to historians, the Romans held two or three banquets every day. But the consumption of so much good food while sitting at a large table two or three times a day must produce in any man, however sturdy his stomach, disorders in the digestive functions. Thus nature has, like you . . ."

" 'Like you' again, what impudence!"

"But they, who studied long and hard simultaneously to enjoy both luxury and exuberant health, considered it vital not only to devour disproportionately large quantities of delicacies but also to maintain the bowels in full working order. They accordingly devised a secret formula . . ."

enthusiastic.

"They invariably took a post-prandial
bath. After the bath, utilizing methods
whose secret has long been lost, they proceeded to vomit up everything they had
swallowed before the bath. Thus were
the insides of their stomachs kept scrupul-
ously clean. Having so cleansed their
stomachs, they would sit down again to
table and there savor to the uttermost the
delicacies of their choice. Then they took
a bath again and vomited once more. In
this way, though they gorged on their
favorite dishes to their hearts' content,
none of their internal organs suffered the
least damage. In my humble opinion,
this was indeed a case of having one's cake
and eating it."

"They certainly seem to have killed two or
more birds with one stone." My master's
expression is one of envy.

"Today, this twentieth century, quite apart
from the heavy traffic and the increased
number of banquets, when our nation is in
the second year of a war against Russia, is
indeed eventful. I consequently firmly
believe that the time has come for us, the
people of this victorious country, to bend
our minds to study of the truly Roman art
of bathing and vomiting. Otherwise, I
am afraid that even the precious people of
this mighty nation will, in the very near
future, become, like you, dyspeptic . . ."

"What, again like me? An annoying fellow", thinks my master.

"Now suppose that we, who are familiar with all things Occidental, by study of ancient history and legend contrive to discover the secret formula that has long been lost; then to make use of it now in our Meiji Era would be an act of virtue. It would nip potential misfortune in the bud and, moreover, it would justify my own everyday life which has been one of constant indulgence in pleasure."

My master thinks all this a trifle odd.

"Accordingly I have now, for some time, been digging into the relevant works of Gibbon, Mommsen and Goldwin Smith but I am extremely sorry to report that, so far, I have gained not even the slightest clue to the secret. However, as you know, I am a man who, once set upon a course, will not abandon it until my object is achieved. Therefore my belief is that a rediscovery of the vomiting method is not far off. I will let you know when it happens. Incidentally, I would prefer postponing that feast of moat-bells and peacocks' tongues which I've mentioned above until the discovery has actually been made. Which would not only be convenient to me but also to you who suffer from a weak stomach."

"So, he's been pulling my leg all along. The style of writing was so sober that I have read it all, and took the whole thing seriously.

Waverhouse must indeed be a man of leisure to play such a practical joke on me," said my master through his laughter.

Several days then passed without any particular event. Thinking it too boring to spend one's time just watching the narcissus in a white vase gradually wither and the slow blossoming in another vase of a branch of the blue-stemmed plum, I have gone round twice to look for Tortoiseshell; but both times unsuccessfully. On the first occasion I thought she was just out, but on my second visit I learnt that she was ill. Hiding myself behind the aspidistra beside a wash-basin, I heard the following conversation which took place between the mistress and her maid on the other side of the sliding paper-door.

"Is Tortoiseshell taking her meal?"

"No, madam, she's eaten nothing this morning. I've let her sleep on the quilt of the foot-warmer, well wrapped up." It does not sound as if they spoke about a cat. Tortoiseshell is being treated as if she were a human.

As I compare this situation with my own lot, I feel a little envious but at the same time I am not displeased that my beloved cat should be treated with such kindness.

"That's bad. If she doesn't eat she will only get weaker."

"Yes indeed, madam. Even me, if I don't eat for a whole day, I couldn't work at all the next day."

The maid answers as though she recognized

the cat as an animal superior to herself. Indeed, in this particular household the cat may well be more important than the maid.

"Have you taken her to see a doctor?"

"Yes, and the doctor was really strange. When I went into his consulting-room carrying Tortoiseshell in my arms, he asked me if I'd caught a cold and tried to take my pulse. I said 'No, Doctor, it is not I who am the patient: this is the patient,' and I placed Tortoiseshell on my knees. The doctor grinned and said he had no knowledge of the sicknesses of cats; and that, if I just left it, perhaps *it* would get better. Isn't he too terrible? I was so angry that I told him, 'Then, please don't bother to examine her: *She* happens to be our precious cat.' And I snuggled Tortoiseshell back into the breast of my kimono and came straight home."

"Truly so."

"Truly so" is one of those elegant expressions that one would never hear in my house. One has to be the thirteenth Shogun's widowed wife's somebody's something to be able to use such a phrase. I was much impressed by its refinement.

"She seems to be sniffling . . ."

"Yes, I'm sure she's got a cold and a sore throat: whenever one has a cold, one suffers from an honorable-cough."

As might be expected from the maid of the thirteenth Shogun's somebody's something, she's quick with honorifics.

"Besides, recently, there's a thing they call consumption . . ."

"Indeed these days one cannot be too careful. What with the increase in all these new diseases like tuberculosis and the black plague."

"Things that did not exist in the days of the Shogunate are all no good to anyone. So you be careful too!"

"Is that so, madam?"

The maid is much moved.

"I don't see how she could have caught a cold: she hardly ever went out . . ."

"No, but you see she's recently acquired a bad friend."

The maid is as highly elated as if she were telling a State secret.

"A bad friend?"

"Yes, that tatty-looking tom at the teacher's house in the main street."

"D'you mean that teacher who makes rude noises every morning?"

"Yes, the one who makes the sounds like a goose being strangled every time he washes his face."

The sound of a goose being strangled is a clever description. Every morning when my master gargles in the bathroom he has an odd habit of making a strange unceremonious noise by tapping his throat with his tooth-brush. When he is in a bad temper he croaks with a vengeance; when he is in a good temper, he gets so pepped up that he croaks even more vigorously. In short, whether he is in a good or a bad temper, he croaks continually and vigorously. According to his wife, until they moved to this house he never had the habit; but he's done it every day since the day he first happened to do it. It is rather a trying habit. We cats cannot even imagine why he should persist in such behavior. Well, let that pass. But what a scathing remark that was about "a tatty-looking tom." I continue to eavesdrop.

"What good can he do making that noise! Under the Shogunate even a lackey or a sandal-carrier knew how to behave; and in a residential quarter there was no-one who washed his face in such a manner."

"I'm sure there wasn't, madam."

That maid is all too easily influenced and she uses "madam" far too often.

"With a master like that, what's to be expected from his cat? It can only be a stray. If he comes round here again, beat him."

"Most certainly I'll beat him. It must be all his fault that Tortoiseshell's so poorly. I'll take it out on him, that I will."

How false these accusations laid against me! But judging it rash to approach too closely, I came home without seeing Tortoiseshell.

When I return, my master is in the study, meditating in the middle of writing something. If I told him what they say about him in the house of the two-stringed harp, he would be very angry: but, as the saying is, ignorance is bliss. There he sits, posing like a sacred poet, groaning.

Just then, Waverhouse, who has expressly

stated in his New Year letter that he would be too busy to call for some long time, dropped in. "Are you composing a new-style poem or something? Show it me if it's interesting."

"I considered it rather impressive prose, so I thought I'd translate it," answers my master somewhat reluctantly.

"Prose? Whose prose?"

"Don't know whose."

"I see, an anonymous author. Among anonymous works, there are indeed some extremely good ones. They are not to be slighted. Where did you find it?"

"The Second Reader," answers my master with imperturbable calmness.

"The Second Reader? What's this got to do with the Second Reader?"

"The connection is that the beautifully written article which I'm now translating appears in the Second Reader."

"Stop talking rubbish. I suppose this is your idea of a last minute squaring of accounts for the peacocks' tongues?"

"I'm not a braggart like you," says my master and twists his mustache. He is perfectly composed.

"Once when someone asked Sanyō whether he'd lately seen any fine pieces of prose, that celebrated scholar of the Chinese classics produced a dunning letter from a packhorse-man and said 'This is easily the finest piece of prose that has recently come to my attention.' Which implies that your eye for the beautiful might, contrary to one's expectations, actually be accurate. Read your piece aloud. I'll review it for you," says Waverhouse as if he were the originator of all aesthetic theories and practice. My master starts to read in the voice of a Zen priest reading that injunction left by the Most Reverend Priest Daitō. "Giant Gravitation," he intoned.

"What on earth is giant gravitation?"

"Giant Gravitation is the title."

"An odd title. I don't quite understand."

"The idea is that there's a giant whose name is Gravitation."

"A somewhat unreasonable idea but, since it's a title, I'll let that pass. All right, carry on with the text. You have a good voice. Which makes it rather interesting."

"Right, but no more interruptions." My master, having laid down his prior conditions, begins to read again.

Kate looks out of the window. Children are playing ball. They throw the ball high up in the sky. The ball rises up and up. After a while the ball comes down. They throw it high again: twice, three times. Every time they throw it up, the ball comes down. Kate asks why it comes down instead of rising up and up. "It is because a giant lives in the earth," replies her mother. "He is the Giant Gravitation. He is strong. He pulls everything toward him. He pulls the houses to the earth. If he didn't they would fly away. Children too would fly away. You've seen the leaves fall, haven't you? That's because the Giant called them. Sometimes you drop a book. It's because the Giant Gravitation asks for it. A ball goes up in the sky. The giant calls for it. Down it falls."

"Is that all?"

"Yes, isn't it good?"

"All right, you win. I wasn't expecting quite such a present in return for the moat-bells."

"It wasn't meant as a return-present or anything like that. I translated it because I thought it was good. Don't you think it's good?" My master stares deep into the gold-rimmed spectacles.

"What a surprise! To think that you of all people had this talent . . . Well, well! I've certainly been taken in right and proper this time. I take my hat off to you." He is alone in his understanding. He's talking to himself. The situation is quite beyond my master's grasp.

"I've no intention of making you doff your cap. I translated this text simply because I thought it was an interesting piece of writing."

"Indeed, yes! Most interesting! Quite as it should be! Smashing! I feel small."

"You don't have to feel small. Since I recently gave up painting in water-colors, I've been thinking of trying my hand at writing."

"And compared with your water-colors, which showed no sense of perspective, no appreciation of differences in tone, your

writings are superb. I am lost in admiration."

"Such encouraging words from you are
making me positively enthusiastic about it,"
says my master, speaking from under his
continuing misapprehension.

Just then Mr. Coldmoon enters with the
usual greeting.

"Why, hello," responds Waverhouse,
"I've just been listening to a terrifically fine
article and the curtain has been rung down
upon my moat-bells." He speaks obliquely
about something incomprehensible.

"Have you really?" The reply is equally
incomprehensible. It is only my master who
seems not to be in any particularly light
humor.

"The other day," he remarked, "a man
called Beauchamp Blowlamp came to see me
with an introduction from you."

"Ah, did he? Beauchamp's an uncommonly honest person but, as he is also somewhat odd, I was afraid that he might make
himself a nuisance to you. However, since
he had pressed me so hard to be introduced
to you . . ."

"Not especially a nuisance . . ."

"Didn't he, during his visit, go on at length
about his name?"

"No, I don't recall him doing so."

"No? He's got a habit at first meeting of
expatiating upon the singularity of his name."

"What is the nature of that singularity?"
butts in Waverhouse, who has been waiting
for something to happen.

"He gets terribly upset if someone pronounces Beauchamp as Beecham."

"Odd!" said Waverhouse, taking a pinch of tobacco from his gold-painted leather tobacco-pouch.

"Invariably he makes the immediate point that his name is not Beecham Blowlamp but Bo-champ Blowlamp."

"That's strange," and Waverhouse inhales pricey tobacco-smoke deep into his stomach.

"It comes entirely from his craze for literature. He likes the effect and is inexplicably proud of the fact that his personal name and his family name can be made to rhyme with each other. That's why when one pronounces Beauchamp correctly, he grumbles that one does not appreciate what he is trying to get across."

"He certainly is extraordinary." Getting more and more interested, Waverhouse hauls back the pipe-smoke from the bottom of his stomach to let it loose at his nostrils. The smoke gets lost en route and seems to be snagged in his gullet. Transferring the pipe to his hand, he coughs chokingly.

"When he was here the other day he said he'd taken the part of a boatman at a meeting of his Reading Society and that he'd got himself laughed at by a gaggle of schoolgirls," says my master with a laugh.

"Ah, that's it, I remember." Waverhouse taps his pipe upon his knees. This strikes me as likely to prove dangerous, so I move a little way farther off. "That Reading Society, now. The other day when I treated him to moat-bells, he mentioned it. He said they were going to make their second meeting a grand affair by inviting well-known literary men, and he cordially invited me to attend. When I asked him if they would again try another of Chikamatsu's dramas of popular life, he said no and that they'd decided on a fairly modern play, *The Golden Demon*. I asked him what role he would take and he said 'I'm going to play O-miya.' Beauchamp as O-miya would certainly be worth seeing. I'm determined to attend the meeting in his support."

"It's going to be interesting, I think." says Coldmoon and he laughs in an odd way.

"But he is so thoroughly sincere and, which is good, has no hint of frivolousness about him. Quite different from Waverhouse, for instance." My master is revenged for Andrea del Sarto, for peacocks' tongues and for moat-bells all in one go. Waverhouse appears to take no notice of the remark.

"Ah well, when all's said and done, I'm nothing but a chopping-board at Gyōtoku."

"Yes, that's about it," observes my master although in fact he does not understand Waverhouse's involved method of describing himself as a highly sophisticated simpleton. But not for nothing has he been so many years a schoolteacher. He is skilled in prevarication, and his long experience in the classrooms can be usefully applied at such awkward moments in his social life.

"What is a chopping-board at Gyōtoku?"

asks the guileless Coldmoon. My master looks toward the alcove and pulverizes that chopping-board at Gyōtoku by saying "Those narcissi are lasting well. I bought them on my way home from the public baths toward the end of last year."

"Which reminds me," says Waverhouse, twirling his pipe, "that at the end of last year I had a really most extraordinary experience."

"Tell us about it." My master, confident that the chopping-board is now safely back in Gyōtoku, heaves a sigh of relief. The Extraordinary Experience of Mr. Waverhouse fell thus upon our ears:

"If I remember correctly it was on the twenty-seventh of December. Beauchamp had said he would like to come and hear me talk upon matters literary and had asked me to be sure to be in. Accordingly, I waited for him all the morning but he failed to turn up. I had lunch and was seated in front of the stove reading one of Pain's humorous books when a letter arrived from my mother in Shizuoka. She, like all old women, still thinks of me as a child. She gives me all sorts of advice; that I mustn't go out at night when the weather's cold; that unless the room is first well-heated by a stove, I'll catch my death of cold every time I take a tub. We owe much to our parents. Who but a parent would think of me with such solicitude? Though normally I take things lightly and as they come, I confess that at that juncture the letter affected me deeply. For it struck me that to idle my life away, as indeed I do, was rather a waste. I felt that I must win honor for my family by producing a masterwork of literature or something like that. I felt I would like the name of Doctor Waverhouse to become renowned, that I should be acclaimed as a leading figure in Meiji literary circles, while my mother is still alive. Continuing my perusal of the letter, I read, 'You are indeed lucky. While our young people are suffering great hardships for the country in the war against Russia, you are living in happy-go-lucky idleness as if life were one long New Year's party organized for your particular benefit!' Actually I'm not as idle as my mother thinks. But she then proceeded to list the names of my class-mates at elementary school who had either died or been wounded in the present war. As, one after another, I read those names, the world grew hollow, all human life quite futile. And she ended her letter by saying 'since I am getting old, perhaps this New Year's rice-cakes will be my last . . .' You will understand that, as she wrote so very dishearteningly, I grew more and more depressed. I began to yearn for Beauchamp to come soon, but somehow he didn't. And at last it was time for supper. I thought of writing in reply to my mother and I actually wrote about a dozen lines. My mother's letter was more than six feet long but, unable myself to match such a prodigious performance, I usually excuse myself after writing some ten lines. As I had been sitting

down for the whole of the day, my stomach
felt strange and heavy. Thinking that if Beauchamp did turn up he could jolly well wait, I
went out for a walk to post my letter. Instead of going toward Fujimichō which is my
usual course, I went, without my knowing it,
out toward the Third Embankment. It was
a little cloudy that evening and a dry wind
was blowing across from the other side of the
moat. It was terribly cold. A train coming
from the direction of Kagurazaka passed
with a whistle along the lower part of the
bank. I felt very lonely. The end of the
year, those deaths on the battlefield, senility,
life's insecurity, that time and tide wait for no
man and other thoughts of a similar nature
ran round in my head. One often talks
about hanging oneself. But I was beginning
to think that one could be tempted to commit
suicide just at such a time as this. It so happened that at that moment I raised my head
slightly and, as I looked up to the top of the
bank, I found myself standing right below
that very pine-tree."

"That very pine-tree? What's that?" cuts
in my master.

"The pine for hanging heads" says Waverhouse ducking his noddle.

"Isn't the pine for hanging heads that one
at Kōnodai?" Coldmoon amplifies the ripple.

"The pine at Kōnodai is the pine for
hanging temple bells. The pine at Dote-
sambanchō is the one for hanging heads.
The reason why it has acquired this name is

that an old legend says that anyone who finds himself under this pine-tree is stricken with a desire to hang himself. Though there are several dozen pine-trees on the bank, every time someone hangs himself, it is invariably on this particular tree that the body is found dangling. I can assure you there are at least two or three such danglings every year. It would be unthinkable to go and dangle on any other pine. As I stared at the tree I noted that a branch stuck out conveniently toward the pavement. Ah! what an exquisitely fashioned branch. It would be a real pity to leave it as it is. I wish so much that I could arrange for some human body to be suspended there. I look around to see if anyone is coming. Unfortunately no one comes. It can't be helped. Shall I hang myself? No, no, if I hang myself, I'll lose my life. I won't because it's dangerous. But I've heard a story that an ancient Greek used to entertain banquet-parties by giving demonstrations of how to hang oneself. A man would stand on a stool and the very second that he put his head through a noose, a second man would kick the stool from under him. The trick was that the first man would loosen the knot in the rope just as his stool was kicked away, and so drop down unharmed. If this story is really true, I've no need to be frightened. So thinking I might try the trick myself, I place my hand on the branch and find it bends in a manner precisely appropriate. Indeed the way it bends

is positively aesthetic. I feel extraordinarily
happy as I try to picture myself floating on
this branch. I felt I simply must try it, but
then I began to think that it would be incon-
siderate if Beauchamp were waiting for me.
Right, I would first see Beauchamp and have
the chat I'd promised: thereafter I could
come out again. So thinking, I went home."

"And is that the happy ending to your
story?" asks my master.

"Very interesting," says Coldmoon with a
broad grin.

"When I got home, Beauchamp had not
arrived. Instead, I found a postcard from
him saying that he was sorry he could not
keep our appointment because of some pres-
sing but unexpected happening and that he
was looking forward to having a long inter-
view with me in the near future. I was
relieved, and I felt happy; for now I could
hang myself with an easy mind. Accordingly, I hurry back to the same spot, and
then . . ." Waverhouse, assuming a nonchalant air, gazes at Coldmoon and my
master.

"And then, what happened?" My master
is becoming a little impatient.

"We've now come to the climax," says
Coldmoon as he twists the strings of his
surcoat.

"And then, somebody had beaten me to it
and had already hanged himself. I'm afraid
I missed the chance just by a second. I see
now that I had been in the grip of the God of

Death. William James, that eminent philosopher, would no doubt explain that the region of the dead in the world of one's subliminal consciousness and the real world in which I actually exist must have interacted in mutual response in accordance with some kind of law of cause and effect. But it really was extraordinary, wasn't it?" Waverhouse looks quite demure.

My master, thinking that he has again been taken in, says nothing but crams his mouth with bean-jam cake and mumbles incoherently.

Coldmoon carefully rakes smooth the ashes in the brazier and casts down his eyes, grinning; but eventually he opens his mouth. He speaks in an extremely quiet tone.

"It is indeed so strange that it does not seem a thing likely to happen. On the other hand, because I myself have recently had a similar kind of experience, I can readily believe it."

"What! Did you too want to stretch your neck?"

"No, mine wasn't a hanging matter. It seems all the more strange in that it also happened at the end of last year at about the same time and on the same day as the Extraordinary Experience of Mr. Waverhouse."

"That's interesting," says Waverhouse. And he, too, stuffs his mouth with bean-jam cake.

"On that day, there was a year-end party combined with a concert given at the house of a friend of mine at Mukōjima. I went there taking my violin with me. It was a grand affair with fifteen or sixteen young or married ladies. Everything was so perfectly arranged that one felt it was the most brilliant event of recent times. When the dinner and the concert were over, we sat and talked till late and, as I was about to take my leave, the wife of a certain doctor came up to me and asked in whisper if I knew that Miss O was unwell. A few days earlier, when last I saw Miss O, she had been looking well and normal. So I was surprised to hear this news, and my immediate questions elicited the information that she had become feverish on the very evening of the day when I'd last seen her and that she was saying all sorts of curious things in her delirium. What was worse, every now and again in that delirium, she was calling my name."

Not only my master but even Waverhouse refrain from making any such hackneyed remark as "You lucky fellow." They just listen in silence.

"They fetched a doctor who examined her. According to the doctor's diagnosis, though the name of the disease was unknown, the high fever affecting the brain made her condition dangerous unless the administration of soporifics worked as effectively as was to be hoped for. As soon as I heard this news, a feeling of something awful grew within me. It was a heavy feeling, as though one were having a nightmare, and all the surrounding air seemed suddenly to be solidifying like a clamp upon my body. On my way home, moreover, I found I could think of nothing else; and it hurt. That beautiful, that gay, that so healthy Miss O . . ."

"Just a minute, please. You've mentioned Miss O about twice. If you've no objection, we'd like to know her name. Wouldn't we?" asks Waverhouse turning to look at my master. The latter evades the question and says "Hmm."

"No, I won't tell you her name since it might compromise the person in question."

"Do you then propose to recount your entire story in such vague, ambiguous, equivocal and noncommittal terms?"

"You mustn't sneer. This is a serious story. Anyway, the thought of that young lady suffering from so odd an ailment filled my heart with mournful emotion and my mind with sad reflections on the ephemerality of life. I felt suddenly depressed beyond all saying, as if every last ounce of my vitality had, just like that, evaporated from my body. I staggered on, tottering and wobbling, till I came to the Azuma Bridge. As I look down, leaning on the parapet, the black waters—at neap or ebb, I don't know which—seem to be coagulating; only just to be moving. A rickshaw coming from the direction of Hana-kawado ran over the bridge. I watched its lamp grow smaller and smaller till it disappeared at the Sapporo Beer factory. Again I look down at the water. And at that moment I

heard a voice from upstream calling my name.
It is most improbable that anyone should be
calling after me at this unlikely time of night
and, wondering whom it could possibly be,
I peered down to the surface of the water,
through it even, but I could see nothing in the
darkness. Thinking it must have been my
imagination, I had decided to go home when
I again heard the voice calling my name. I
stood dead-still and listened. When I heard
it calling me for the third time, though I was
gripping the parapet firmly, my knees began
to tremble uncontrollably. The voice seemed to be coming either from far away or from
the bottom of the river, but it was unmis-
takably the voice of Miss O. In spite of
myself I answered 'Yes.' My answer was so
loud that it echoed back from the still water
and, surprised by my own voice, I looked
around me in a startled manner. There was
no one to be seen. No dog. No moon.
Nothing. At this very second I experienced
a sudden urge to immerse myself in that total
darkness from which the voice had sum-
moned me. And, once again, the voice of
Miss O pierced my ears painfully, appealingly,
as if begging for help. This time I cried 'I'm
coming now' and, leaning well out over the
parapet, I looked down into the somber
depths. For, it seemed to me that the sum-
moning voice was surging powerfully up from
beneath the waves. Thinking that the source
of the pleading must lie in the water directly
below me, I at last managed to clamber onto

the parapet. I was determined that, next time the voice called out to me, I would dive straight in; and, as I stood watching the stream, once again the thin thread of that pitiful voice came floating up to me. This, I thought, is it; and, jumping high with all my strength, I came dropping down without regret like a pebble or something."

"So you actually did dive in?" asks my master, blinking his eyes.

"I never thought you'd go as far as that," says Waverhouse pinching the tip of his nose.

"After my dive I became unconscious, and for a while I seemed to be living in a dream. But eventually I woke up and, though I felt cold, I was not at all wet and did not feel as if I had swallowed any water. Yet I was sure that I had dived. How very strange! Realizing that something peculiar must have taken place, I looked around me and received a real shock. I'd meant to dive into the water but apparently I'd accidentally landed in the middle of the bridge itself. I felt abysmally regretful. Having, by sheer mistake, jumped backwards instead of forwards, I'd lost my chance to answer the summons of the voice." Coldmoon smirks and fiddles with the strings of his surcoat as if they were in some way irksome.

"Ha-ha-ha, how very comical. It's odd that your experience so much resembles mine. It, too, could be adduced in support of the theories of Professor James. If you were to write it up in an article entitled 'The Human

Response,' it would astound the whole literary world. But what," persisted Waverhouse,
"became of the ailing Miss O?"

"When I called at her house a few days ago
I saw her, just inside the gate, playing battledore and shuttlecock with her maid. So I
expect she has completely recovered from her
illness."

My master, who for some time has been
deep in thought, finally opens his mouth and,
in a spirit of unnecessary rivalry, remarks
"I too have a strange experience to relate."

"You've got what?" In Waverhouse's
view, my master counts for so little that he is
scarcely entitled to have experiences.

"Mine also occurred at the end of last
year."

"It's queer," observed Coldmoon, "that all
our experiences took place toward the end of
last year"; and he sniggers. A piece of bean-
jam cake adheres to the corner of his chipped
front tooth.

"And it took place, doubtless," added
Waverhouse, "at the very same time on the
very same day."

"No, I think the date is different: it was
about the 20th. My wife had earlier asked
me, as a year's-end present to herself, to take
her to hear Settsu Daijō. I'd replied that I
wouldn't say no, and asked her the nature of
the program for that day. She consulted
the newspapers and answered that it was one
of Chikamatsu's suicide dramas, *Unagidani*.
'Let's not go today; I don't like *Unagidani*,'

122

I Am a Cat

said I. So we did not go that day. Next day, my wife, bringing out the newspaper again, said 'Today he's doing the *Monkey Man at Horikawa*; so, let's go'. I said let's not, because *Horikawa* was so frivolous, just *samisen*-playing with no meat in it. My wife went away looking discontented. The following day, she stated almost as a demand, 'Today's program is *TheTemple With Thirty-Three Pillars*. You may dislike the *Temple* quite as strongly as you disliked all the others; but since the treat is intended to be for me, surely you won't object to taking me there'. 'If you've set your heart on it so firmly, then we'll go: but since the performance has been announced as Settsu's farewell appearance on the stage, the house is bound to be packed full and since we haven't booked in advance, it will obviously be impossible to get in. To start with, in order to attend such performances there's an established procedure to be observed. You have to go to the theatre-teahouse and there negotiate for seat-reservations. It would be hopeless to try going about it in the wrong way. You just can't dodge this proper procedure. So, sorry though I am, we simply cannot go today.' My wife's eyes glittered fiercely. 'Since I am a mere woman, I do not understand your complicated procedures; but both Ōhara's mother and Kimiyo of the Suzuki family managed to get in without observance of any such formalities; and they heard everything very well. I realize that you are a teacher, but surely you

don't have to go through all that troublesome
rigmarole just to visit a theatre? It's too
bad . . . you are so . . .' and her voice became
tearful. I gave in. 'All right. We'll go to
the theatre even if we can't get into it. After
an early supper we'll take the tram.' 'If
we're going, we must be there by four o'clock:
so we mustn't dilly-dally.' She suddenly
became quite lively. When I asked her why
one had to be there by four o'clock, she explained that Kimiyo had told her that, if one
arrived any later, all the seats would be taken.
I asked her again, to make quite sure, if it
would be fruitless to turn up later than four
o'clock; and she answered briskly 'Of course
it would be no good.' Then, d'you know, at
that very moment the shivering set in."

"Do you mean your wife?" asks Coldmoon.

"Oh, no, my wife was as fit as a fiddle. It
was I. I had a sudden feeling that I was
shriveling like a pricked balloon. Then I
grew giddy and unable even to move."

"You were taken ill with a most remarkable
suddenness," commented Waverhouse.

"This is terrible. What shall I do? I'd
like so much to grant my wife her wish, her
one and only request in the whole long year.
All I ever do is scold her fiercely or not speak
to her or nag her about household expenses or
insist that she cares more carefully for the
children; and yet I have never rewarded her
for all her efforts in the domestic field.
Today, luckily, I have the time and the money

available. I could easily take her on some little outing. And she very much wants to go. Just as I very much want to take her. But much indeed as I want to take her, this icy shivering and frightful giddiness make it impossible for me even to step down from the entrance of my own house, let alone to climb up into a tram. The more I think how deeply I grieve for her, the poor thing, the worse my shivering grows and the more giddy I become. I thought if I consulted a doctor and took some medicine, I might get well before four o'clock. I discussed the matter with my wife and sent for Mr. Amaki, Bachelor of Medicine. Unfortunately he had been on night duty at the university hospital and hadn't yet come home. However we received every assurance that he was expected home by about two o'clock and that he would hurry round to see me the minute he returned. What a nuisance. If only I could get some sedative, I know I could be cured before four. But when luck is running against one, nothing goes well. Here I am, just this once in a long long time, looking forward to seeing my wife's happy smile and to be sharing in that happiness. My expectations seem sadly unlikely to be fulfilled. My wife, with a most reproachful look, enquires whether it really is impossible for me to go out. 'I'll go; certainly I'll go. Don't worry, I'm sure I'll be all right by four. Wash your face, get ready to go out and wait for me.' Though I uttered all these reassurance, my mind was shaken

with profound emotions. The chill shivering
strengthens and accelerates, and my giddiness
grows worse and worse. Unless I do get well
by four o'clock and implement my promise,
one can never tell what such a pusillanimous
woman might do. What a wretched business.
What should I do. As I thought it possible
that the very worst could happen, I began to
consider whether perhaps it might be my duty
as a husband to explain to my wife, now while
I was still in possession of my faculties, the
dread truths concerning mortality and the
vicissitudes of life. For if the worst should
happen, she would then at least be prepared
and less liable to be overcome by the par-
oxysms of her grief. I accordingly sum-
moned my wife to come immediately to my
study. But when I began by saying 'Though
but a woman you must be aware of that
Western proverb which states that there is
many a slip 'twixt the cup and the lip,' she
flew into a fury. 'How should I know anything at all about such sideways-written
words? You're deliberately making a fool
of me by choosing to speak English when you
know perfectly well that I don't understand a
word of it. All right. So I can't understand
English. But if you're so besotted about
English, why didn't you marry one of those
girls from the mission schools? I've never
come across anyone quite so cruel as you.'
In the face of this tirade, my kindly feelings,
my husbandly anxiety to prepare her for ex-
tremities, were naturally damped down. I'd

like you two to understand that it was not out of malice that I spoke in English. The words sprang solely from a sincere sentiment of love for my wife. Consequently my wife's malign interpretation of my motives left me feeling helpless. Besides, my brain was somewhat disturbed by reason of the cold shivering and the giddiness: and, on top of all that, I was understandably distraught by the effort of trying quickly to explain to her the truths of mortality and the nature of the vicissitudes of life. That was why, quite unconsciously and forgetting that my wife could not understand the tongue, I spoke in English. I immediately realized I was in the wrong. It was all entirely my fault. But as a result of my blunder, the cold shivering intensified its violence and my giddiness grew ever more viciously vertiginous. My wife, in accordance with my instructions, proceeds to the bathroom and, stripping herself to the waist, completes her make-up. Then, taking a kimono from a drawer, she puts it on. Her attitudes make it quite clear that she is now ready to go out any time, and is simply waiting for me. I begin to get nervous. Wishing that Mr. Amaki would arrive quickly, I look at my watch. It's already three o'clock. Only one hour to go. My wife slides open the study-door and, putting her head in, asks 'Shall we go now?' It may sound silly to praise one's own wife, but I had never thought her quite so beautiful as she was that moment. Her skin, thoroughly polished with soap, gleams deliciously and makes a marvelous

contrast with the blackness of her silken surcoat. Her face has a kind of radiance both
externally and shining from within; partly
because of the soap and partly because of her
intense longing to listen to Settsu Daijō. I
feel I must, come what may, take her out to
satisfy that yearning. All right, perhaps I
will make the awful effort to go out. I was
smoking and thinking along these lines when
at long last Mr. Amaki arrived. Excellent.
Things are turning out as one would wish.
However, when I told him about my condition, Amaki examined my tongue, took my
pulse, tapped my chest, stroked my back,
turned my eyelids inside out, patted my skull
and thereafter sank into deep thought for quite
some time. I said to him 'It is my impression
that there may be some danger . . .'; but he
replied 'No, I don't think there's anything
seriously wrong.' 'I imagine it would be
perfectly all right for him to go out for a little
while?' asked my wife. 'Let me think.'
Amaki sank back into the profundities of
thought, reemerging to remark 'Well, so long
as he doesn't feel unwell . . .' 'O but I do
feel unwell,' I said. 'In that case I'll give you
a mild sedative and some liquid medicine . . .'
'Yes please. This is going to be something
serious, isn't it?' 'Oh no, there's nothing to
worry about. You mustn't get nervous,'
said Amaki; and thereupon departed. It is
now half past three. The maid was sent to
fetch the medicine. In accordance with my
wife's imperative instructions, the wretched
girl not only ran the whole way there but also

the whole way back. It is now a quarter to four. Fifteen minutes still to go. Then, quite suddenly, just about that time, I began to feel sick. It came on with a quite extraordinary suddenness. All totally unexpected. My wife had poured the medicine into a teacup and placed it in front of me but, as soon as I tried to lift the teacup, some keck-keck thing stormed up from within the stomach. I am compelled to put the teacup down. 'Drink it up quickly' urges my wife. Yes, indeed; I must drink it quickly and go out quickly. Mustering all my courage to imbibe the potion, I bring the teacup to my lips when again that insuppressible keck-keck thing prevents my drinking it. While this process of raising the cup and putting it down is being several times repeated, the minutes crept on till the wall-clock in the living-room struck four o'clock. Ting-ting-ting-ting. Four o'clock it is. I can no longer dilly-dally and I raise the teacup once again. D'you know, it really was most strange. I'd say that it was certainly the uncanniest thing I've ever experienced. At the fourth stroke my sickliness just vanished, and I was able to take the medicine without any trouble at all. And by about ten past four—here I must add that I now realized for the first time how truly skilled a physician we have in Dr. Amaki— the shivering of my back and the giddiness in my head both disappeared like a dream. Up to that point I had expected that I was bound to be laid up for days but, to my great pleasure, the illness proved to have been completely cured."

"And did you two then go out to the theatre?" asks Waverhouse with the puzzled expression of one who cannot see the point of a story.

"We certainly both wanted to go but, since it had been my wife's reiterated view that there was no hope of getting in after four o'clock, what could we do? We didn't go. If only Amaki had arrived fifteen minutes earlier, I could have kept my promise and my wife would have been satisfied. Just that fifteen-minute difference. I was indeed distressed. Even now, when I think how narrow was the margin, I am again distressed."

My master, having told his shabby tale, contrives to look like a person who has done his duty. I imagine he feels he's got even with the other two.

"How very vexing," says Coldmoon. His laugh, as usual, displays his broken tooth.

Waverhouse, with a false naivety, remarks as if to himself. "Your wife, with a husband so thoughtful and kind-hearted, is indeed a lucky woman." Behind the sliding paper-door, we heard the master's wife make an harumphing noise as though clearing her throat.

I had been quietly listening to the successive stories of these three precious humans, but I was neither amused nor saddened by what I'd heard. I merely concluded that human beings were good for nothing except for the

strenuous employment of their mouths for
the purpose of whiling away their time in
laughter at things which are not funny and in
the enjoyment of amusements which are not
amusing. I have long known of my master's
selfishness and narrow-mindedness; but, because he usually has little to say, there was always something about him which I could not
understand. I'd felt a certain caution, a
certain fear, even a certain respect toward
him on account of that aspect of his nature
which I did not understand. But having
heard his story, my uncertainties suddenly
coalesced into a mere contempt for him. Why
can't he listen to the stories of the other two
in silence? What good purpose can he serve
by talking such utter rubbish just because his
competitive spirit has been roused? I wonder if, in his portentous writings, Epictetus
advocated any such course of action. In
short, my master, Waverhouse and Coldmoon
are all like hermits in a peaceful reign. Though
they adopt a nonchalant attitude, keeping
themselves aloof from the crowd, segegrated
like so many snake-gourds swayed lightly by
the wind, in reality they, too, are shaken by
just the same greed and worldly ambition as
their fellow-men. The urge to compete and
their anxiety to win are revealed flickeringly
in their everyday conversation, and only a
hair's breadth separates them from the Phil-
istines whom they spend their idle days de-
nouncing. They are all animals from the same
den. Which fact, from a feline viewpoint, is
infinitely regrettable. Their only moderately

redeeming feature is that their speech and
conduct are less tediously uninventive than
those of less subtle creatures.

As I thus summed up the nature of the
human race, I suddenly felt the conversation
of these specimens to be intolerably boring;
so I went round to the garden of the mistress
of the two-stringed harp to see how Tortoiseshell was getting on. Already the pine-tree
decorations for the New Year and that season's sacred festoons have been taken down.
It is the 10th of January. From a deep sky
containing not even a single streak of cloud
the glorious springtime sun shines down upon
the lands and seas of the whole wide world,
so that even her tiny garden seems yet more
brilliantly lively than when it saw the dawn
of New Year's Day. There is a cushion on
the veranda, the sliding paper-door is closed
and there's nobody about. Which probably
means that the mistress has gone off to the
public baths. I'm not at all concerned if the
mistress should be out, but I do very much
worry about whether Tortoiseshell is any
better. Since everything's so quiet and not
a sign of a soul, I hop up onto the veranda
with my muddy paws and curl up right in the
middle of the cushion. Which I find com-
fortable. A drowsiness came over me and,
forgetting all about Tortoiseshell, I was about
to drop off into a doze when suddenly I heard
voices beyond the paper-door.

"Ah, thanks. Was it ready?" The mistress has not gone out after all.

"Yes, madam. I'm sorry to have taken

such a long time. When I got there, the man who makes Buddhist altar-furniture told me he'd only just finished it."

"Well, let me see it. Ah, but it's beautifully done. With this, Tortoiseshell can surely rest in peace. Are you sure the gold won't peel away?"

"Yes, I've made sure of it. They said that, as they had used the very best quality, it would last longer than most human memorial tablets. They also said that the character for 'honor' in Tortoiseshell's posthumous name would look better if written in the cursive style, so they had added the appropriate strokes."

"Is that so? Well, let's put Myōyoshinnyo's tablet in the family shrine and offer incense sticks."

Has anything happened to Tortoiseshell? Thinking something must be wrong, I stand up on the cushion. Ting! "Amen! Myōyoshinnyo. Save us, merciful Buddha! May she rest in peace." It is the voice of the mistress.

"You, too, say prayers for her."

Ting! "Amen! Myōyoshinnyo. Save us, merciful Buddha! May she rest in peace." Suddenly my heart throbs violently. I stand dead-still upon the cushion; like a wooden cat; not even my eyes are moving.

"It really was a pity. It was only a cold at first."

"Perhaps if Dr. Amaki had given her some medicine, it might have helped."

"It was indeed Amaki's fault. He paid too little regard to Tortoiseshell."

"You must not speak ill of other persons. After all, everyone dies when their allotted span is over."

It seems that Tortoiseshell was also attended by that skilled physician, Dr. Amaki.

"When all's said and done, I believe the root-cause was that the stray cat at the teacher's in the main street took her out too often."

"Yes, that brute has done for Tortoiseshell."

I would like to exculpate myself but, realizing that at this juncture it behoves me to be patient, I swallow hard and continue listening. There is a pause in the conversation.

"Life does not always turn out as one wishes. A beauty like Tortoiseshell dies young. That ugly stray remains healthy and flourishes in devilment . . ."

"It is indeed so, Madam. Even if one searched high and low for a cat as charming as Tortoiseshell, one would never find another person like her."

She didn't say 'another cat': she said 'another person.' The maid seems to think that cats and human beings are of one race. Which reminds me that the face of this particular maid is strangely like a cat's.

"If only instead of our dear Tortoiseshell..."

"That wretched stray at the teacher's had been taken, then, Madam, how perfectly everything would have gone . . ."

If everything had gone that perfectly, I

would have been in deep trouble. Since I have not yet had the experience of being dead, I cannot say whether or not I would like it. But the other day, it happening to be unpleasantly chilly, I crept into the tub for conserving half-used charcoal and settled down upon its still-warm contents. The maid, not realizing I was in there, popped on the lid. I shudder even now at the mere thought of the agony I then suffered. According to Miss Blanche, the cat across the road, one dies if that agony continues for even a very short stretch. I wouldn't complain if I were asked to substitute for Tortoiseshell; but if one cannot die without going through that kind of agony, I frankly would not care to die on anyone's behalf.

"Though a cat, she had her funeral service conducted by a priest and now she's been given a posthumous Buddhist name. I don't think she would expect us to do more."

"Of course not, madam. She is indeed thrice blessed. The only comment that one might make is that the funeral service read by the priest was, perhaps, a little wanting in gravity."

"Yes, and I though it rather too brief. But when I remarked to the priest from the Gekkei Temple 'you've finished very quickly, haven't you?' he answered 'I've done sufficient of the effective parts; quite enough to get a kitty into Paradise'."

"Dear me! . . . But if the cat in question were that unpleasant stray . . . "

I have pointed out often enough that I have no name, but this maid keeps calling me "that stray." She is a vulgar creature.

"So very sinful a creature, Madam, would never be able to rest in peace, however many edifying texts were read for its salvation."

I do not know how many hundreds of times I was thereafter stigmatized as a stray. I stopped listening to their endless babble while it was still only half-run and, slipping down from the cushion, I jumped off the veranda. Then, simultaneously erecting every single one of my eighty-eight thousand eight hundred and eighty hairs, I shook my whole body. Since that day I have not ventured near the mistress of the two-stringed harp. No doubt by now she herself is having texts of inadequate gravity read on her behalf by the priest from the Gekkei Temple.

Nowadays I haven't even energy to go out. Somehow life seems weary. I have become as indolent a cat as my master is an indolent human. I have come to understand that it is only natural that people should so often explain my master's self-immurement in his study as the result of a love-affair gone wrong.

As I have never caught a rat, that O-san person once proposed that I should be expelled; but my master knows that I'm no ordinary common-or-garden cat, and that is why I continue to lead an idle existence in this house. For that understanding I am deeply grateful to my master. What's more, I take every opportunity to show the respect due to his perspicacity. I do not get particularly angry with O-san's ill-treatment of me, for she does not understand why I am as I now am. But when, one of these days, some master-sculptor, some regular Hidari Jingorō, comes and carves my image on a temple-gate; when some Japanese equivalent of the French master-portraitist, Steinlein, immortalizes my features on a canvas, then at last will the silly purblind beings in shame regret their lack of insight.

III

TORTOISESHELL is dead; one cannot consort with Rickshaw Blacky; and I feel a little lonely. Luckily I have made acquaintances among humankind so I do not suffer from any real sense of boredom. Someone wrote recently asking my master to have my photograph taken and the picture sent to him. And then the other day somebody else presented some millet dumplings, that speciality of Okayama, specifically addressed to me. The more that humans show me sympathy, the more I am inclined to forget that I am a cat. Feeling that I am now closer to humans than to cats, the idea of rallying my own race in an effort to wrest supremacy from the bipeds no longer has the least appeal. Moreover, I have developed, indeed evolved, to such an extent that there are now times when I think of myself as just another human in the human world. Which I find very encouraging. It is not that I look down on my own race: but it is no more than natural to feel most at ease among those whose attitudes are similar to one's own. I would consequently feel somewhat piqued if my growing penchant for mankind were stigmatized as fickleness or flippancy or treachery. It is precisely those who sling such words about in slanderous attacks on others who are usually both drearily strait-laced and born unlucky. Having thus graduated from felinity to humanity, I find myself no longer able to confine my interests to the world of Tortoiseshell and Blacky. With an haughtiness not less prideful than that of human beings, I, too, now like to judge and criticize their thoughts and words and deeds. This, surely, is equally natural. Yet, though I have become thus proudly conscious of my own dignity, my master still regards me as a cat only slightly superior to any other common-or-garden moggy. For, as if they were his own and without so much as a by-your-leave to me, he has eaten all the millet dumplings. Which is, I find, regrettable. Nor does he seem yet to have dispatched my photograph. I suppose I would be justified if I made this fact a cause for grumbling; but after all, if our opinions—my master's and mine—are naturally at difference, the consequences of that difference cannot be helped. Since I am seeking to behave with total humanity, I'm finding it increasingly difficult to write about the activities of cats with whom I no longer associate. I must accordingly seek the indulgence of my readers if I now confine my writing to reports about such respected figures as Waverhouse and Coldmoon.

Today is a Sunday and the weather fine. The master has therefore crept out of his study

and, placing a brush, an inkstone and a
writing pad in a row before him, he now lies
flat on his belly beside me; and is groaning
hard. I watch him, thinking that he is perhaps making this peculiar noise in the birth-
pangs of some literary effort. After a while
and in thick black strokes he wrote "Burn
incense." Is it going to be a poem or a
haiku? Just when I was thinking that the
phrase was rather too witty for my master, he
abandons it and, his brush running quickly
over the paper, writes an entirely new line:
"Now for some little time I have been thinking of writing an article about Mr. the-late-
and-sainted Natural Man." At this point
the brush stops dead. My master, brush in
hand, racks his brains, but no bright notions
seem to emerge for he now starts licking the
head of his brush. I watched his lips acquire
a curious inkiness. Then, underneath what
he had just written, he drew a circle, put in
two dots as eyes, added a nostrilled nose in
the center and finally drew a single sideways
line for a mouth. One could not call such
creations either *haiku* or prose. Even my
master must have been disgusted with himself, for he quickly smeared away the face.
He then starts a new line. He seems to have
some vague notion that, provided he himself
produces a new line, maybe some kind of a
Chinese poem will evolve itself. After further moonings, he suddenly started writing
briskly in the colloquial style. "Mr. the-late-
and-sainted Natural Man is one who studies

Infinity, reads the Analects of Confucius, eats baked yams and has a running nose." A somewhat muddled phrase. He thereupon read the phrase aloud in a declamatory manner and, quite unlike his usual self, laughed. "Ha-ha-ha. Interesting! But that 'running nose' is a shade cruel, so I'll cross it out"; and he proceeds to draw lines across that phrase. Though a single line would clearly have sufficed, he draws two lines and then three lines. He goes on drawing more and more lines regardless of their crowding into the neighboring line of writing. When he has drawn eight such obliterations, he seems unable to think of anything to add to his opening outburst. So he takes to twirling his mustache. Determined to wring some telling sentence from his whiskers, he is still twisting them up and twirling them down when his wife appears from the living-room and, sitting herself down immediately before my master's nose, remarks "My dear."

"What is it?" My master's voice sounds dully like a gong struck under water. His wife seems not to like the answer, for she starts all over again. "My dear!" she says.

"Well, what is it?" This time, cramming a thumb and index finger into a nostril, he yanks out nostril-hairs.

"We are a bit short, this month . . . "

"Couldn't possibly be short. We've settled the doctor's fee and we paid off the bookshop's bill last month. So this month, there ought in fact to be something left over." He

coolly examines his uprooted nostril-hairs as
though they were some wonder of the world.

"But because you, instead of eating rice,
have taken to bread and jam . . ."

"Well, how many tins of jam have I gone
through?"

"This month, eight tins were emptied."

"Eight? I certainly haven't eaten that
much."

"It wasn't only you. The children also
lick it."

"However much one licks, one couldn't
lick more than two or three shillings' worth."
My master calmly plants his nostril-hairs,
one by one, on the writing pad. The sticky-
rooted bristles stand upright on the paper like
a little copse of needles. My master seems
impressed by this unexpected discovery and
he blows upon them. Being so sticky, they
do not fly away.

"Aren't they obstinate?" he says and blows
upon them frantically.

"It is not only the jam. There's other
things we have to buy." The lady of the
house expresses her extreme dissatisfaction by
pouting sulkily.

"Maybe." Again inserting his thumb and
finger, he extracts some hairs with a jerk.
Among these hairs of various hue, red ones
and black ones, there is a single pure white
bristle. My master who, with a look of great
surprise, has been staring at this object,
proceeds to show it to his wife, holding it up
between his fingers right in front of her face.

"No, don't." She pushes his hand away
with a grimace of distaste.

"Look at it! A white hair from the
nostrils." My master seems to be immensely
impressed. His wife, resigned, went back
into the living-room with a laugh. She
seems to have given up hope of getting any
answer to her problems of domestic economy.
My master resumes his consideration of the
problems of Natural Man.

Having succeeded in driving off his wife
with his scourge of nostril-hair, he appears to
feel relieved; and, while continuing that de-
pilation, struggles to get on with his article.
But his brush remains unmoving. "That
'eats baked yams' is also superfluous. Out
with it." He deletes the phrase. "And
'incense burns' is somewhat over-abrupt, so
let's cross that out too." His exuberant
self-criticism leaves nothing on the paper but
the single sentence "Mr. the-late-and-sainted
Natural Man is one who studies Infinity and
reads the Analects of Confucius." My master thinks this statement a trifle over-simpli-
fied. "Ah well, let's not be bothered: let's
abandon prose and just make it an inscrip-
tion." Brandishing the brush crosswise, he
paints vigorously on the writing pad in that
water-color style so common among literary
men and produces a very poor study of an
orchid. Thus all his precious efforts to write
an article have come down to this mere nothing. Turning the sheet, he writes something
that makes no sense. "Born in Infinity,

At this moment Waverhouse drifts into the
room in his usual casual fashion. He appears to make no distinction between his own
and other people's houses; for unannounced
and unceremoniously, he enters any house
and, what's more, will sometimes float in
unexpectedly through a kitchen-door. He is
one of those who, from the moment of their
birth, dis-caul themselves of all such tiresome
things as worry, reserve, scruple and concern.

"Giant Gravitation again?" asks Waverhouse still standing.

"How could I be always writing only about
Giant Gravitation? I'm trying to compose
an epitaph for the tombstone of Mr. the-late-
and-sainted Natural Man," replied my master
with considerable exaggeration.

"Is that some sort of posthumous Buddhist
name like Accidental Child?" inquires
Waverhouse in his usual irrelevant style.

"Is there then someone called Accidental
Child?"

"No, of course there isn't; but I take it that
you're working on something like that."

"I don't think Accidental Child is anyone I
know.   But Mr. the-late-and-sainted Natural
Man is a person of your own acquaintance."

"Who on earth could get a name like that?"

"It's Sorosaki. After he graduated from
the University, he took a postgraduate course
involving study of the 'theory of infinity.'
But he overworked, got peritonitis and died

of it. Sorosaki happened to be a very close friend of mine."

"All right, so he was your very close friend. I'm far from criticizing that fact. But who was responsible for converting Sorosaki into Mr. the-late-and-sainted Natural Man?"

"Me. I created that name. For there is really nothing more philistine than the posthumous names conferred by Buddhist priests." My master boasts as if his nomination of Natural Man were a feat of artistry.

"Anyway, let's see the epitaph," says Waverhouse laughingly. He picks up my master's manuscript and reads it out aloud. "Eh . . . 'Born into infinity, studied infinity and died into infinity. Mr. the-late-and-sainted Natural Man. Infinity.' I see. This is fine. Quite appropriate for poor old Sorosaki."

"Good, isn't it?" says my master obviously very pleased.

"You should have this epitaph engraved on a weight-stone for pickles and then leave it at the back of the main hall of some temple for the practice-benefit of passing weight-lifters. It's good. It's most artistic. Mr. the-late-and-sainted may now well rest in peace."

"Actually, I'm thinking of doing just that," answers my master quite seriously. "But you'll have to excuse me," he went on, "I won't be long. Just play with the cat. Don't go away." And my master departed like the wind without even waiting for Waverhouse to answer.

Being thus unexpectedly required to enter-

tain the culture-vulture Waverhouse, I cannot
very well maintain my sour attitude. Accordingly I mew at him encouragingly and
sidle up on to his knees. "Hello," says
Waverhouse, "you've grown distinctly chub-
by. Let's take a look at you." Grabbing
me impolitely by the scruff of my neck he
hangs me up in mid-air. "Cats like you that
let their hind legs dangle are cats that catch
no mice . . . Tell me," he said, turning to my
master's wife in the next room, "has he ever
caught anything?"

"Far from catching so much as a single
mouse, he eats rice-cakes and then dances."
The lady of the house unexpectedly probes my
old wound. Which embarrassed me. Especially when Waverhouse still held me in
mid-air like a circus-performer.

"Indeed, with such a face, it's not surprising that he dances. Do you know, this cat
possesses a truly insidious physionomy. He
looks like one of those goblin-cats illustrated
in the old story-books." Waverhouse, bab-
bling whatever comes into his head, tries to
make conversation with the mistress. She
reluctantly interrupts her sewing and comes
into the room.

"I do apologize. You must be bored. He
won't be long now." And she poured fresh
tea for him.

"I wonder where he's gone."

"Heaven only knows. He never explains
where he's going. Probably to see his doctor."

"You mean Dr. Amaki? What a mis-

fortune for Amaki to be involved with such a
patient."

Perhaps finding this comment difficult to
answer, she answers briefly: "Well, yes."

Waverhouse takes not the slightest notice,
but goes on to ask "How is he lately? Is his
weak stomach any better?"

"It's impossible to say whether it's better
or worse. However carefully Dr. Amaki
may look after him, I don't see how his health
can ever improve if he continues to consume
such vast quantities of jam." She thus works
off on Waverhouse her earlier grumblings to
my master.

"Does he eat all that much jam? It sounds
like a child."

"And not just jam. He's recently taken to
guzzling grated radish on the grounds that
it's a sovereign cure for dyspepsia."

"You surprise me," marvels Waverhouse.

"It all began when he read in some rag
that grated radish contains diastase."

"I see. I suppose he reckons that grated
radish will repair the ravages of jam. It's
certainly an ingenious equation." Waverhouse seems vastly diverted by her recital of
complaint.

"Then only the other day he forced some
on the baby."

"He made the baby eat jam?"

"No, grated radish! Would you believe
it? He said 'Come here, my little babykin:
father'll give you something good . . .' Whenever, once in a rare while, he shows affection
for the children, he always does remarkably

silly things. A few days ago he put our
second daughter on top of a chest of drawers."

"What ingenious scheme was that?"
Waverhouse looks to discover ingenuities in
everything.

"There was no question of any ingenious
scheme. He just wanted the child to make
the jump when it's quite obvious that a little
girl of three or four is incapable of such
tomboy feats."

"I see. Yes, that proposal does indeed
seem somewhat lacking in ingenuity. Still,
he's a good man without an ill wish in his
heart."

"Do you think that I could bear it if, on
top of everything else, he were ill-natured?"
She seems in uncommonly high spirits.

"Surely you don't have cause for such
vehement complaint? To be comfortably off
as you are is, after all, the best way to be.
Your husband neither leads the fast life nor
squanders money on dandified clothing.
He's a born family man of quiet taste."
Waverhouse fairly lets himself go in unac-
customed laud of an unknown way of life.

"On the contrary, he's not at all like
that. . . "

"Indeed? So he has secret vices? Well,
one cannot be too careful in this world."
Waverhouse offers a nonchalantly fluffy comment.

"He has no secret vices, but he is totally
abandoned in the way he buys book after
book, never to read a single one. I wouldn't
mind if he used his head and bought in

moderation. But no. Whenever the mood takes him, he ambles off to the biggest bookshop in the city and brings back home as many books as chance to catch his fancy. Then, at the end of the month, he adopts an attitude of complete detachment. At the end of last year, for instance, I had a terrible time coping with the bill that had been accumulating month after month."

"It doesn't matter that he should bring home however many books he may like. If, when the bill-collector comes, you just say that you'll pay some other time, he'll go away."

"But one cannot put things off indefinitely." She looks cast down.

"Then you should explain the matter to your husband and ask him to cut down expenditure on books."

"And do you really believe he would listen to me? Why, only the other day, he said 'You are so unlike a scholar's wife: you lack the least understanding of the value of books. Listen carefully to this story from ancient Rome. It will give you beneficial guidance for your future conduct.'"

"That sounds interesting. What sort of story was it?" Waverhouse becomes enthusiastic, though he appears less sympathetic to her predicament than prompted by sheer curiosity.

"It seems there was in ancient Rome a king named Tarukin."

"Tarukin? That sounds odd in Japanese."

"I can never remember the names of foreigners. It's all too difficult. Maybe he was a barrel of gold. He was, at any rate, the seventh king of Rome."

"Really? The seventh barrel of gold sounds certainly queer. But, tell me, what then happened to this seventh Tarukin."

"You mustn't tease me like that. You quite embarrass me. If you know this king's true name, you should teach me it. Your attitude," she snaps at him, "is really most unkind."

"I tease you? I wouldn't dream of doing such an unkind thing. It was simply that the seventh barrel of gold sounded so wonderful. Let's see . . . a Roman, the seventh king . . . I can't be absolutely certain but I rather think it must have been Tarquinius Superbus, Tarquin the Proud. Well, it doesn't really matter who it was. What did this monarch do?"

"I understand that some woman, Sibyl by name, went to this king with nine books and invited him to buy them."

"I see."

"When the king asked her how much she wanted, she stated a very high price; so high that the king asked for a modest reduction. Whereupon the woman threw three of the nine books into the fire where they were quickly burnt to ashes."

"What a pity!"

"The books were said to contain pro-phecies, predictions, things like that of which there was no other record anywhere."

"Really?"

"The king, believing that six books were bound to be cheaper than nine, asked the price of the remaining volumes. The price proved to be exactly the same; not one penny less. When the king complained of this outrageous development, the women threw another three books into the fire. The king apparently still hankered for the books and he accordingly asked the price of the last three left. The woman again demanded the same price as she had asked for the original nine. Nine books had shrunk to six, and then to three, but the price remained unaltered even by a farthing. Suspecting that any attempt to bargain would merely lead the woman to pitch the last three volumes into the flames, the king bought them at the original staggering price. My husband appeared confident that, having heard this story, I would begin to appreciate the value of books; but I don't at all see what it is that I'm supposed to have learnt to appreciate."

Having thus stated her own position, she as good as challenges Waverhouse to contravert her. Even the resourceful Waverhouse seems to be at a loss. He draws a handkerchief from the sleeve of his kimono and tempts me to play with it. Then, in a loud voice as if an idea had suddenly struck him, he remarked "But you know, Mrs. Sneaze, it is precisely because your husband buys so many books and fills his head with wild notions that he is occasionally mentioned as a scholar or something of that sort. Only the other day a comment on your husband appeared in a literary magazine."

"Really?" She turns round. After all, it's only natural that his wife should feel anxiety about comments on my master. "What did it say?"

"Oh, only a few lines. It said that Mr. Sneaze's prose was like a cloud that passes in the sky, like water flowing in a stream."

"Is that," she asks smiling, "all that it said?"

"Well, it also said 'it vanishes as soon as it appears and, when it vanishes, it is forever forgetful to return.'"

The lady of the house looks puzzled and asks anxiously "Was that praise?"

"Well, yes, praise of a sort," says Waverhouse coolly as he jiggles his handkerchief in front of me.

"Since books are essential to his work, I suppose one shouldn't complain; but his eccentricity is so pronounced that . . ."

Waverhouse assumes that she's adopting a new line of attack. "True," he interrupts, "he is a little eccentric: but any man who pursues learning tends to get like that." His answer, excellently noncommittal, contrives to combine ingratiation and special pleading.

"The other day, when he had to go somewhere soon after he got home from school, he found it too troublesome to change his clothes. So do you know, he sat down on his low desk without even taking off his overcoat and ate his dinner just as he was. He had his tray put on the footwarmer while I sat on the floor holding the rice-container. It was really very funny . . ."

"It sounds like the olde-tyme custom when generals sat down to identify the severed heads of enemies killed in battle. But that would be quite typical of Mr. Sneaze. At any rate he's never boringly conventional." Waverhouse offers a somewhat strained compliment.

"A woman cannot say what's conventional or unconventional, but I do think his conduct is often unduly odd."

"Still, that's better than being conventional." As Waverhouse moves firmly to the support of my master, her dissatisfaction deepens.

"People are always saying this or that is conventional, but would you please tell what makes a thing conventional?" Adopting a defiant attitude, she demands a definition of conventionality.

"Conventional? When one says something is conventional . . . It's a bit difficult to explain . . ."

"If it's so vague a thing, surely there's nothing wrong with being conventional." She begins to corner Waverhouse with typically feminine logic.

"No, it isn't vague. It's perfectly clearcut. But it's hard to explain."

"I expect you call everything you don't

like conventional." Though totally uncal-
culated, her words land smack on target.
Waverhouse is now indeed cornered and can
no longer dodge defining the conventional.

"I'll give you an example. A conventional
man is one who would yearn after a girl of
sixteen or eighteen but, sunk in silence, never
do anything about it; a man who, whenever
the weather's fine, would do no more than
stroll along the banks of the Sumida taking,
of course, a flask of *sake* with him."

"Are there really such people?" Since she
cannot make head or tail of the twaddle
vouchsafed by Waverhouse, she begins to
abandon her position; which she finally
surrenders by saying "It's all so complicated
that it's really quite beyond me."

"You think that complicated? Imagine
fitting the head of Major Pendennis onto
Bakin's torso, wrapping it up and leaving it
all for one or two years exposed to European
air."

"Would that produce a conventional
man?" Waverhouse offers no reply but
merely laughs.

"In fact it could be produced without going
to quite so much trouble. If you added a
shop-assistant from a leading store to any
middle-school student and divided that sum
by two, then indeed you'd have a fine example of a conventional man."

"Do you really think so?" She looks
puzzled but certainly unconvinced.

"Are you still here?" My master sits

himself down on the floor beside Waverhouse. We had not noticed his return.

" 'Still here' is a bit hard. You said you wouldn't be long and you yourself invited me to wait for you."

"You see, he's always like that," remarks the lady of the house leaning toward Waverhouse.

"While you were away I heard all sorts of tales about you."

"The trouble with women is that they talk too much. It would be good if human beings would keep as silent as this cat." And the master strokes my head.

"I hear you've been cramming grated radish into the baby."

"Hum," says my master and laughs. He then added "Talking of the baby, modern babies are quite intelligent. Since that time when I gave our baby grated radish, if you ask him 'where is the hot place?' he invariably sticks out his tongue. Isn't it strange?"

"You sound as if you were teaching tricks to a dog. It's positively cruel. By the way, Coldmoon ought to have arrived by now."

"Is Coldmoon coming?" asks my master in a puzzled voice.

"Yes. I sent him a postcard telling him to be here not later than one o'clock."

"How very like you! Without even asking us if it happened to be convenient. What's the idea of asking Coldmoon here?"

"It's not really my idea, but Coldmoon's own request. It seems he is going to give a lecture to the Society of Physical Science. He said he needed to rehearse his speech and asked me to listen to it. Well, I thought it would be obliging to let you hear it too. Accordingly I suggested he should come to your house. Which should be quite convenient since you are a man of leisure. I know you never have any engagements. You'd do well to listen." Waverhouse thinks he knows how to handle the situation.

"I wouldn't understand a lecture on physical science," says my master in a voice betraying his vexation at his friend's high-handed action.

"On the contrary, his subject is no such dry-as-dust matter as, for example, the magnetized nozzle. The transcendentally extraordinary subject of his discourse is 'The Mechanics of Hanging.' Which should be worth listening to."

"Inasmuch as you once only just failed to hang yourself, I can understand your interest in the subject; but I'm . . ."

". . . The man who got cold shivers over going to the theatre; so you cannot expect not to listen to it." Waverhouse interjects one of his usual flippant remarks and Mrs. Sneaze laughs. Glancing back at her husband, she goes off into the next room. My master, keeping silent, strokes my head. This time, for once, he stroked me with delicious gentleness.

Some seven minutes later in comes the anticipated Coldmoon. Since he's due to

give his lecture this same evening, he is not
wearing his usual get-up. In a fine frock-coat
and with a high and exceedingly white clean
collar, he looks twenty per cent more hand-
some than himself. "Sorry to be late." He
greets his two seated friends with perfect
composure.

"It's ages that we've now been waiting for
you. So we'd like you to start right away.
Wouldn't we?" says Waverhouse, turning to
look at my master. The latter, thus forced
to respond, somewhat reluctantly says
"Hmm." But Coldmoon's in no hurry. He
remarks "I think I'll have a glass of water,
please."

"I see you are going to do it in real style.
You'll be calling next for a round of ap-
plause." Waverhouse, but he alone, seems
to be enjoying himself.

Coldmoon produced his text from an inside
pocket and observed "Since it is the established practice, may I say I would welcome
criticism." That invitation made, he at last
begins to deliver his lecture.

"Hanging as a death-penalty appears to
have originated among the Anglo-Saxons.
Previously, in ancient times, hanging was
mainly a method of committing suicide. I
understand that among the Hebrews it was
customary to execute criminals by stoning
them to death. Study of the Old Testament
reveals that the word 'hanging' is there used to
mean 'suspending a criminal's body after
death for wild beasts and birds of prey to

devour it.' According to Herodotus, it would seem that the Jews, even before they departed from Egypt, abominated the mere thought that their dead bodies might be left exposed at night. The Egyptians used to behead a criminal, nail the torso to a cross and leave it exposed during the night. The Persians . . ."

"Steady on, Coldmoon," Waverhouse interrupts. "You seem to be drifting farther and farther away from the subject of hanging. Do you think that wise?"

"Please be patient. I am just coming to the main subject. Now, with respect to the Persians. They, too, seemed to have used crucifixion as a method of criminal execution. However, whether the nailing took place while the criminal was alive or simply after his death is not incontrovertibly established."

"Who cares? Such details are really of little importance," yawned my master as from boredom.

"There are still many matters of which I'd like to inform you but, as it will perhaps prove tedious for you . . ."

" 'As it might prove' would sound better than 'as it will perhaps prove.' What d'you think, Sneaze?" Waverhouse starts carping again but my master answers coldly "What difference could it make?"

"I have now come to the main subject, and will accordingly recite my piece."

"A storyteller 'recites a piece.' An orator

should use more elegant diction." Waverhouse again interrupts.

"If to 'recite my piece' sounds vulgar, what words should I use?" asks Coldmoon in a voice that showed he was somewhat nettled.

"It is never clear, when one is dealing with Waverhouse, whether he's listening or interrupting. Pay no attention to his heckling, Coldmoon: just keep going." My master seeks to find a way through the difficulty as quickly as possible.

"So having made your indignant recitation, now I suppose you've found the willow tree?" With a pun on a little-known *haiku* Waverhouse, as usual, comes up with something odd. Coldmoon, in spite of himself, broke into laughter.

"My researches reveal that the first account of the employment of hanging as a deliberate means of execution occurs in the Odyssey. Volume Twenty-Two. The relevant passage records how Telemachus arranged the execution by hanging of Penelope's twelve ladies-in-waiting. I could read the passage aloud in its original Greek but, since such an act might be regarded as an affectation, I will refrain from doing so. You will, however, find the passage between lines 465 and 473."

"You'd better cut out all that Hellenic stuff. It sounds as if you are just showing off your knowledge of Greek. What do you think, Sneaze?"

"On that point I agree with you. It would be more modest, altogether an improvement, to avoid such ostentation." Quite unusually my master immediately sides with Waver-house. The reason is, of course, that neither can read a word of Greek.

"Very well, I will this evening omit those references. And now I will recite . . . that is to say, I will now continue. Let us consider, then, how a hanging is actually carried out. One can envisage two methods. The first method is that adopted by Telemachus who, with the help of Eumaeus and Philoetios, tied one end of a rope to the top of a pillar: next, having made several loose loops in the rope, he forced a woman's head through each such loop, and finally hauled up hard on the other end of the rope."

"In short, he had the women dangling in a row like shirts hung out at a laundry. Right?"

"Exactly. Now the second method is, as in the first case, to tie one end of a rope to the top of a pillar and similarly to secure the other end of the rope somewhere high up on the ceiling. Thereafter several other short ropes are attached to the main rope, and in each of these subsidiary ropes a slip-knot is then tied. The women's heads are then inserted in the slip-knots. The idea is that at the crucial moment you remove the stools on which the women have been stood."

"They would then look something like those ball-shaped paper-lanterns one some-times sees suspended from the end-tips of rope-curtains. Wouldn't they?" hazarded Waverhouse.

"That I cannot say," answered Coldmoon cautiously. "I have never seen any such ball as a paper-lantern-ball: but if such balls exist, the resemblance may be just. Now, the first method as described in the Odyssey is, in fact, mechanically impossible; and I shall proceed, for your benefit, to substantiate that statement."

"How interesting," says Waverhouse.

"Indeed, most interesting," adds my master.

"Let us suppose that the women are to be hanged at intervals of an equal distance; and that the rope between the two women nearest the ground stretches out horizontally. Right? Now $\alpha1$, $\alpha2$ up to $\alpha6$ become the angles between the rope and the horizon. T_1, T_2 and so on up to T_6 represent the force exerted on each section of the rope, so that $T_7 = X$ is the force exerted on the lowest part of the rope. W is, of course, the weight of the women. So far so good. Are you with me?"

My master and Waverhouse exchange glances, and say "Yes, more or less." I need hardly point out that the value of this "more or less" is singular to Waverhouse and my master. It could possibly have a different value for other people.

"Well, in accordance with the theory of averages as applied to the polygon, a theory with which you must of course be well acquainted, the following twelve equations can, in this particular case, be established:

$T_1 \cos \alpha1 = T_2 \cos \alpha2$......(1)
$T_2 \cos \alpha2 = T_3 \cos \alpha3$......(2)"

"I think that's enough of the equations," my master irresponsibly remarks.

"But these equations are the very essence of my lecture." Coldmoon really seems reluctant to be parted from them.

"In that case, let's hear those particular parts of its very essence at some other time." Waverhouse, too, seems out of his depth.

"But if I omit the full detail of the equations, it becomes impossible to substantiate the mechanical studies to which I have devoted so much effort . . ."

"Oh, never mind that. Cut them all out," came the cold-blooded comment of my master.

"That's most unreasonable. However, since you insist, I will omit them."

"That's good," says Waverhouse, unexpectedly clapping his hands.

"Now we come to England where, in *Beowulf*, we find the word 'gallows': that is to say 'galga.' It follows that hanging as a penalty must have been in use as early as the period with which the book is concerned. According to Blackstone, a convicted person who is not killed at his first hanging by reason of some fault in the rope should simply be hanged again. But, oddly enough, one finds it stated in *The Vision of Piers Plowman* that even a murderer should not be strung up twice. I do not know which statement is correct, but there are many melancholy instances of victims failing to be killed outright. In 1786 the authorities attempted to hang a notorious villain named Fitzgerald but, by some strange chance, when the stool was removed, the rope broke. At the next attempt the rope proved so long that his legs touched ground and he again survived. In the end, at the third attempt, he was enabled to die with the help of the spectators."

"Well, well," says Waverhouse becoming, as was only to be expected, re-enlivened.

"A true thanatophile." Even my master shows signs of jollity.

"There is one other interesting fact. A hanged person grows taller by about an inch. This is perfectly true. Doctors have measured it."

"That's a novel notion. How about it, Sneaze?" says Waverhouse turning to my master. "Try getting hanged. If you were an inch taller, you might acquire the appearance of an ordinary human being." The reply, however, was delivered with an unexpected gravity.

"Tell me, Coldmoon, is there any chance of surviving that process of extension by one inch?"

"Absolutely none. The point is that it is the spinal cord which gets stretched in hanging. It's more a matter of breaking than of growing taller."

"In that case, I won't try." My master abandons hope.

There was still a good deal of the lecture left to deliver and Coldmoon had clearly been anxious to deal with the question of the physiological function of hanging. But

Waverhouse made so many and such capri-
ciously-phrased interjections and my master
yawned so rudely and so frequently that
Coldmoon finally broke off his rehearsal in
mid-flow; and took his leave. I cannot tell
you what oratorical triumphs he achieved,
still less what gestures he employed that
evening, because the lecture took place miles
away from me.

A few days passed uneventfully by. Then,
one day about two in the afternoon, Waverhouse dropped in with his usual casual man-
ners and looking as totally uninhibited as his
own concept of the "Accidental Child."
The minute he sat down he asked abruptly
"Have you heard about Beauchamp Blowlamp and the Takanawa Incident?" He
spoke excitedly, in a tone of voice appropriate
to an announcement of the fall of Port
Arthur.

"No, I haven't seen him lately." My
master is his usual cheerless self.

"I've come today, although I'm busy,
especially to inform you of the frightful
blunder which Beauchamp has committed."

"You're exaggerating again. Indeed you're
quite impossible."

"Impossible, never: improbable, perhaps.
I must ask you to make a distinction on this
point, for it affects my honor."

"It's the same thing," replied my master
assuming an air of provoking indifference.
He is the very image of a Mr. the-late-and-
sainted Natural Man.

"Last Sunday, Beauchamp went to the

Sengaku Temple at Takanawa. Which was silly in this cold weather, especially when to make such a visit nowadays stamps one as a country bumpkin out to see the sights."

"But Beauchamp's his own master. You've no right to stop him going."

"True, I haven't got the right; so let's not bother about that. The point is that the temple-yard contains a show-room displaying relics of the forty-seven rōnin. Do you know it?"

"N-no."

"You don't? But surely you've been to the Temple?"

"No."

"Well, I am surprised. No wonder you so ardently defended Beauchamp. But it's positively shameful that a citizen of Tokyo should never have visited the Sengaku Temple."

"One can contrive to teach without trailing out to the ends of the city." My master grows more and more like his blessed Natural Man.

"All right. Anyway, Beauchamp was examining the relics when a married couple, Germans as it happened, entered the show-room. They began by asking him questions in Japanese: but, as you know, Beauchamp is always aching to practice his German so he naturally responded by rattling off a few words in that language. Apparently he did it rather well. Indeed, when one thinks back over the whole deplorable incident, his very

"Well, what happened?" My master final-ly succumbs.

"The Germans pointed out a gold-lac-quered pill-box which had belonged to Ōtaka Gengo and, saying they wished to buy it, asked Beauchamp if the object were for sale. Beauchamp's reply was not uninteresting. He said such a purchase would be quite im-possible because all Japanese people were true gentlemen of the sternest integrity. Up to that point he was doing fine. However, the Germans, thinking that they'd found a useful interpreter, thereupon deluged him with questions."

"About what?"

"That's just it. If he had understood their questions, there would have been no trouble. But you see he was subjected to floods of such questions, all delivered in rapid German, and he simply couldn't make head or tail of what was being asked. When at last he chanced to understand part of their outpourings, it was something about a fireman's axe or a mallet—some word he couldn't translate—so again, naturally, he was completely at a loss how to reply."

"That I can well imagine," sympathizes my master, thinking of his own difficulties as a teacher.

"Idle onlookers soon began to gather round and eventually Beauchamp and the Germans were totally surrounded by staring eyes. In his confusion Beauchamp fell to blushing.

In contrast to his earlier self-confidence he was now at his wit's end."

"How did it all turn out?"

"In the end Beauchamp could stand it no longer, shouted *Sainara* in Japanese and came rushing home. I pointed out to him that *Sainara* was an odd phrase to use and inquired whether, in his home-district, people used *sainara* rather than *sayonara*. He replied they would say *sayonara* but, since he was talking to Europeans, he had used *sainara* in order to maintain harmony. I must say I was much impressed to find him a man mindful of harmony even when in difficulties."

"So that's the bit about *sainara*. What did the Europeans do?"

"I hear that the Europeans looked utterly flabbergasted." And Waverhouse gave vent to laughter. "Interesting, eh?"

"Frankly, no. I really can't find anything particularly interesting in your story. But that you should have come here specially to tell me the tale, that I do find much more interesting." My master taps his cigarette's ash into the brazier. Just at that moment the bell on the lattice-door at the entrance rang with an alarming loudness, and a piercing woman's voice declared "Excuse me." Waverhouse and my master look at each other in silence.

Even while I am thinking that it is unusual for my master's house to have a female visitor, the owner of that piercing voice enters the room. She is wearing two layers of silk crepe kimono, and looks to be a little over forty. Her forelock towers up above the bald expanse of her brow like the wall of a dyke and sticks out toward heaven for easily one half the length of her face. Her eyes, set at an angle like a road-cut through a mountain, slant up symmetrically in straight lines. I speak, of course, metaphorically. Her eyes, in fact, are even narrower than those of a whale. But her nose is exceedingly large. It gives the impression that it has been stolen from someone else and thereafter fastened in the center of her face. It is as if a large stone-lantern from some major shrine had been moved to a tiny ten-square-meter garden. It certainly asserts its own importance, but yet looks out of place. It could almost be termed hooked: for it begins by jutting sharply out but then, halfway along its length, it suddenly turns shy so that its tip, bereft of the original vigour, hangs limply down to peer into the mouth below. Her nose is such that, when she speaks, it is the nose rather than the mouth which seems to be in action. Indeed, in homage to the enormity of that organ, I shall refer hence forward to its owner as Madam Conk. When the ceremonials of her self-introduction had been completed, she glared around the room and remarked "What a nice house."

"What a liar," says my master to himself, and concentrates upon his smoking. Waverhouse studies the ceiling. "Tell me," he says, "is that odd pattern the result of a rain-leak or is it inherent in the grain of the wood?"

"Rain-leak, naturally" replies my master. To which Waverhouse coolly answers "Wonderful."

Madam Conk clearly regards them as unsociable persons and boils quietly with suppressed annoyance. For a time the three of them just sit there in a triangle without saying a word.

"I've come to ask you about a certain matter." Madam Conk starts up again.

"Ah." My master's response lacks warmth.

Madam Conk, dissatisfied with this development, bestirs herself again. "I live nearby. In fact, at the residence on the corner of the block across the road."

"That large house in the European style, the one with a godown? Ah, yes. Of course. Have I not seen 'Goldfield' on the nameplate of that dwelling?" My master, at last, seems ready to take cognizance of Goldfield's European house and his incorporated godown; but his attitude toward Madam Conk displays no deepening of respect.

"Of course my husband should call upon you and seek your valued advice, but he is always so busy with his company affairs." She puts on a "that ought to shift them" face, but my master remains entirely unimpressed. He is, in fact, displeased by her manner of speaking, finding it too direct in a woman met for the first time. "And not of just one

company either. He is connected with two
or three of them. And is a director of them
all. As, I expect, you already know." She
looks as if saying to herself "Now surely he
should feel small." In point of fact, the
master of this house behaves most humbly
toward anyone who happens to be a doctor
or a professor; but, oddly enough, he offers
scant respect toward businessmen. He
considers a middle-school teacher to be a
more elevated person than any businessman.
Even if he doesn't really believe this, he is
quite resigned, being of an unadaptable nature, to the fact that he can never hope to be
smiled upon by businessmen or millionaires.
For he feels nothing but indifference toward
any person, no matter how rich or influential,
from whom he has ceased to hope for bene-
fits. He consequently pays not the faintest
attention to anything extraneous to the society
of scholars, and is almost actively disinter-
ested in the goings-on of the business world.
Had he even the vaguest knowledge of the
activities of businessmen, he still could never
muster the slightest feeling of awe or respect
for such abysmal persons. While, for her
part, Madam Conk could never stretch her
imagination to the point of considering that
any being so eccentric as my master could actually exist, that any corner of the world
might harbor such an oddity. Her experience
has included meetings with many people and
invariably, as soon as she declares that she
is wife to Goldfield, their attitude toward her

never fails immediately to alter. At any party whatsoever and no matter how lofty the social standing of any man before whom she happens to find herself, she has always found that Mrs. Goldfield is eminently acceptable. How then could she fail to impress such an obscure old teacher? She had expected that the mere mention of the fact that her house was the corner residence of the opposite block would startle my master even before she added information about Mr. Goldfield's notable activities in the world of business.

"Do you know anyone called Goldfield?" my master inquires of Waverhouse with the utmost nonchalance.

"Of course I know him. He's a friend of my uncle. Only the other day he was present at our garden party." Waverhouse answers in a serious manner.

"Really?" said my master. "And who, may I ask, is your uncle?"

"Baron Makiyama," replied Waverhouse in even graver tones. My master is obviously about to say something but, before he can bring himself to words, Madam Conk turns abruptly toward Waverhouse and subjects him to a piercing stare. Waverhouse, secure in a kimono of the finest silk, remains entirely unperturbed.

"Oh, you are Baron Makiyama's . . . That I didn't know. I hope you'll excuse me . . . I've heard so much about Baron Makiyama from my husband. He tells me that the

Baron has always been so helpful..."
Madam Conk's manner of speech has suddenly become polite. She even bows.

"Ah yes," observes Waverhouse who is
inwardly laughing. My master, quite asto-
nished, watches the two in silence.

"I understand he has even troubled the
Baron about our daughter's marriage..."

"Has he indeed?" exclaims Waverhouse as
if surprised. Even Waverhouse seems somewhat taken aback by this unexpected development.

"We are, in fact, receiving proposal after
proposal in respect of marriage to our daughter. They flood in from all over the place.
You will appreciate that, having to think
seriously of our social position, we cannot
rashly marry off our daughter to just anyone..."

"Quite so." Waverhouse feels relieved.

"I have, in point of fact, made this visit
precisely to raise with you a question about
this marriage matter." Madam Conk turns
back to my master and reverts to her earlier
vulgar style of speech. "I hear that a certain
Avalon Coldmoon pays you frequent visits.
What sort of a man is he?"

"Why do you want to know about Coldmoon?" replies my master in a manner
revealing his displeasure.

"Perhaps it is in connection with your
daughter's marriage that you wish to know
something about the character of Coldmoon," puts in Waverhouse tactfully.

"If you could tell me about his character, it would indeed be helpful."

"Then is it that you want to give your daughter in marriage to Coldmoon?"

"It's not a question of my wanting to give her." Madam Conk immediately squashes my master. "Since there will be innumerable proposals, we couldn't care less if he doesn't marry her."

"In that case, you don't need any information about Coldmoon," my master replies with matching heat.

"But you've no reason to withhold information." Madam Conk adopts an almost defiant attitude.

Waverhouse, sitting between the two and holding his silver pipe as if it were an umpire's instrument of office, is secretly beside himself with glee. His gloating heart urges them on to yet more extravagant exchanges.

"Tell me, did Coldmoon actually say he wanted to marry her?" My master fires a broadside pointblank.

"He didn't actually say he wanted to, but . . ."

"You just think it likely that he might want to?" My master seems to have realized that broadsides are best in dealing with this woman.

"The matter is not yet so far advanced, but . . . well, I don't think Mr. Coldmoon is wholly averse to the idea." Madam Conk rallies well in her extremity.

"Is there any concrete evidence whatsoever that Coldmoon is enamored of this daughter of yours?" My master, as if to say "now answer me if you can," sticks out his chest belligerently.

"Well, more or less, yes." This time my master's militance has failed in its effect. Waverhouse has hitherto been so delighted with his self-appointed role of umpire that he has simply sat and watched the scrap; but now his curiosity seems suddenly to have been aroused. He puts down the pipe and leans forward. "Has Coldmoon sent your daughter a love-letter? What fun! One more new event since the New Year and, at that, a splendid subject for debate." Waverhouse alone is pleased.

"Not a love-letter. Something much more ardent than that. Are you two really so much in the dark?" Madam Conk adopts a disbelieving attitude.

"Are you aware of anything?" My master, looking nonplussed, addresses himself to Waverhouse.

Waverhouse takes refuge in banter. "I know nothing. If anyone should know, it would be you." His reaction is disappointingly modest.

"But the two of you know all about it." Madam Conk triumphs over both of them.

"Oh!" The sound expressed their simultaneous astonishment.

"In case you've forgotten, let me remind

you of what happened. At the end of last year Mr. Coldmoon went to a concert at the Abe residence in Mukōjima. Right? That evening, on his way home, something happened at Azuma Bridge. You remember? I won't repeat the details since that might compromise the person in question, but what I've said is surely proof enough. What do you think?" She sits bolt-upright with her diamond-ringed fingers in her lap. Her magnificent nose looks more resplendent than ever: so much so that Waverhouse and my master seem practically obliterated.

My master, naturally, but even Waverhouse also, appear dumbfounded by this surprise attack. For a while they just sit there in bewilderment, like patients whose fits of ague have suddenly ceased. But as the first shock of their astonishment subsides and they come slowly back to normality, their sense of humor irrepressibly asserts itself and they burst into gales of laughter. Madam Conk, baulked in her expectations and ill-prepared for this reaction of rude laughing, glares at both of them.

"Was that your daughter? Isn't it wonderful! You're quite right. Indeed Coldmoon must be mad about her. I say, Sneaze, there's no point now in trying to keep it secret. Let's make a clean breast of everything." My master just says "Hum."

"There's certainly no point in your trying to keep it secret. The cat's already out of the

bag." Madam Conk is once more cock-
ahoop.

"Yes, indeed, we're cornered. We'll have
to make a true statement on everything concerning Coldmoon for this lady's information. Sneaze! you're the host here. Pull
yourself together, man. Stop grinning like
that or we'll never get this business sorted out.
It's extraordinary. Secretiveness is a most
mysterious matter. However well one guards
a secret, sooner or later it's bound to come
out. Indeed, when you come to think of it,
it really is most extraordinary. Tell us, Mrs.
Goldfield, how did you ever discover this
secret? I am truly amazed." Waverhouse
rattles on.

"I've a nose for these things." Madam
Conk declares with some self-satisfaction.

"You must indeed be very well informed.
Who on earth has told you about this matter?"

"The wife of the rickshawman who lives
just there at the back."

"Do you mean that man who owns that vile
black cat?" My master is wide-eyed.

"Yes, your Mr. Coldmoon has cost me a
pretty penny. Every time he comes here I
want to know what he talks about, so I've
arranged for the wife of the rickshawman to
learn what happens and to report it all to
me."

"But that's terrible!" My master raises
his voice.

"Don't worry, I don't give a damn what
you do or say. I'm not in the least concerned
with you. Only with Mr. Coldmoon."

"Whether with Coldmoon or with anyone
else ... Really, that rickshaw woman is a
quite disgusting creature." My master begins
to get angry.

"But surely she is free to stand outside your
hedge. If you don't want your conversa-
tions overheard, you should either talk less
loudly or live in a larger house." Madam
Conk is clearly not the least ashamed of
herself. "And that's not my only source.
I've also heard a deal of stuff from the
Mistress of the two-stringed harp."

"You mean about Coldmoon?"

"Not solely about Coldmoon." This sounds
menacing but, far from retreating in embarrassment, my master retorts. "That woman
gives herself such airs. Acting as though she
and she alone were the only person of any
standing in this neighborhood. A vain, an
idiotic fellow ..."

"Pardon me! It's a woman you're describing. A fellow, did you say? Believe
me, you're talking out of the back of your
neck." Her language more and more betrays
her vulgar origin. Indeed, it now appears as
if she has only come in order to pick a quarrel.
But Waverhouse, typically, just sits listening
to the quarrel as if it were being conducted
for his amusement. Indeed he looks like a
Chinese sage at a cockfight: cool and above
it all.

match Madam Conk in the exchange of
scurrilities, and he lapses into a forced silence.
But eventually a bright idea occurs to him.

"You've been speaking as though it were
Coldmoon who was besotted with your
daughter; but from what I've heard, the situation is quite different.   Isn't that so, Waverhouse?"

"Certainly.   As we heard it, your daughter
fell ill and then, we understand, began bab-
bling in delirium."

"No.   You've got it all wrong."   Madam
Conk gives the lie direct.

"But Coldmoon undoubtedly said that that
was what he had been told by Dr. O's wife."

"That was our trap.   We'd asked the
Doctor's wife to play that trick on Coldmoon
precisely in order to see how he'd react."

"Did the doctor's wife agree to this deception in full knowledge that it was a trick?"

"Yes.   Of course we couldn't expect her
to help us purely for affection's sake.   As I've
said, we've had to lay out a very pretty penny
on one thing and another."

"You are quite determined to impose yourself upon us and quiz us in detail about
Coldmoon, eh?"   Even Waverhouse seems
to be getting annoyed for he uses some sharp-
ish turns of phrase quite unlike his usual
manner.

"Ah well, Sneaze," he continues, "what do
we lose if we talk?   Let's tell her everything.
Now, Mrs. Goldfield, both Sneaze and I will

tell you anything within reason about Coldmoon. But it would be more convenient for
us if you'd present your questions one at a
time."

Madam Conk was thus at last brought to
see reason. And when she began to pose her
questions, her style of speech, only recently
so coarsely violent, acquired a certain civil
polish: at least when she spoke to Waverhouse. "I understand," she opens, "that Mr.
Coldmoon is a bachelor of science. Now
please tell me in what sort of subject has he
specialized?"

"In his post-graduate course, he's studying
terrestrial magnetism," answers my master
seriously.

Unfortunately, Madam Conk does not
understand this answer. Therefore, though
she says "Ah," she looks dubious and asks:
"If one studies that, could one obtain a
doctor's degree?"

"Are you seriously suggesting that you
wouldn't allow your daughter to marry him
unless he held a doctorate?" The tone of
my master's inquiry discloses his deep displeasure.

"That's right. After all, if it's just a bachelor's degree, there are so many of them!"
Madam Conk replies with complete uncon-
cern.

My master's glance at Waverhouse reveals
a deepening disgust.

"Since we cannot be sure whether or not
he'll gain a doctorate, you'll have to ask us

"Is he still just studying that terrestrial something?"

"A few days ago," my master quite innocently offers, "he made a speech on the results of his investigation of the mechanics of hanging."

"Hanging? How dreadful! He must be peculiar. I don't suppose he could ever become a doctor by devoting himself to hanging."

"It would of course be difficult for him to gain a doctorate if he actually hanged himself; but it is not impossible to become a doctor through study of the mechanics of hanging."

"Is that so?" she answers, trying to read my master's expression. It's a sad, sad thing but, since she does not know what mechanics are, she cannot help feeling uneasy. She probably thinks that to ask the meaning of such a trifling matter might involve her in loss of face. Like a fortuneteller, she tries to guess the truth from facial expressions. My master's face is glum. "Is he studying anything else, something more easy to understand?"

"He once wrote a treatise entitled 'A Discussion of the Stability of Acorns in Relation to the Movements of Heavenly Bodies.'"

"Does one really study such things as acorns at a university?"

"Not being a member of any university, I cannot answer your question with complete certainty: but since Coldmoon is engaged in such studies, the subject must undoubtedly be worth studying." With a deadpan face, Waverhouse makes fun of her.

Madam Conk seems to have realized that her questions about matters of scholarship have carried her out of her depth, for she changes the subject. "By the way," she says, "I hear that he broke two of his front teeth when eating mushrooms during the New Year season."

"True; and a rice-cake became fixed on the broken part." Waverhouse, feeling that this question is indeed up his street, suddenly becomes light-hearted.

"How unromantic! I wonder why he doesn't use a toothpick!"

"Next time I see him, I'll pass on your sage advice," says my master with a chuckle.

"If his teeth can be snapped on mushrooms, they must be in very poor condition. What do you think?"

"One could hardly say such teeth were good. Could one, Waverhouse?"

"Of course they can't be good, but they do provide a certain humor. It's odd that he hasn't had them filled. It really is an extraordinary sight when a man just leaves his teeth to become mere hooks for snagging rice-cakes."

"Is it because he lacks the money to get them filled or because he's just so odd that he leaves them unattended to?"

"Ah, you needn't worry. I don't suppose

he will continue as Mr. Broken Front-tooth
for any long time." Waverhouse is evidently
regaining his usual bouyancy.

Madam Conk again changes the subject.
"If you should have some letter or anything
which he's written, I'd like to see it."

"I have masses of postcards from him.
Please have a look at them," and my master
produces some thirty or forty postcards from
his study.

"Oh, I don't have to look at so many of
them . . . perhaps two or three would do . . ."

"Let me choose some for you," offers
Waverhouse, adding, as he selects a picture
postcard, "Here's an interesting one."

"Gracious! So he paints pictures as well?
Rather clever that," she exclaims. But after
examining the picture she remarks "How very
silly! It's a badger! Why on earth does he
have to paint a badger of all things! Strange.
But it does indeed look like a badger." She
is, albeit reluctantly, mildly impressed.

"Read what he's written beside it," suggests my master with a laugh. Madam Conk
begins to read aloud like a servant-girl de-
ciphering a newspaper.

"On New Year's Eve, as calculated under
the ancient calendar, the mountain badgers
hold a garden party at which they dance
excessively. Their song says 'This evening,
being New Year's Eve, no mountain hikers
will come this way.' And bom-bom-bom
they thump upon their bellies. What is he
writing about? Is he not being a trifle fri-

volous?" Madam Conk seems seriously dissatisfied.

"Doesn't this heavenly maiden please you?" Waverhouse picks out another card on which a kind of angel in celestial raiment is depicted as playing upon a lute.

"The nose of this heavenly maiden seems rather too small."

"Oh no, that's about the average size for an angel. But forget the nose for the moment and read what it says," urges Waverhouse.

"It says 'Once upon a time there was an astronomer. One night he went as was his wont high up into his observatory and, as he was intently watching the stars, a beautiful heavenly maiden appeared in the sky and began to play some music; music too delicate ever to be heard on earth. The astronomer was so entranced by the music that he quite forgot the dark night's bitter cold. Next morning the dead body of the astronomer was found covered with pure white frost. An old man, a liar, told me that this story was all true'. What the hell is this? It makes no sense, no nothing. Can Coldmoon really be a bachelor of science? Perhaps he should read a few literary magazines." Thus mercilessly does Madam Conk lambaste the defenseless Coldmoon.

Waverhouse for fun selects a third postcard and says "Well then, what about this one?" The card has a sailing boat printed on it and, as usual, there is something scribbled underneath the picture.

Last night a tiny whore of sixteen summers
Declared she had no parents.
Like a plover on a reefy coast,
She wept on waking in the early morning.
Her parents, sailors both, lie at the bottom
of the sea.

"Oh, that's good. How very clever! He's
got real feeling," erupted Madam Conk.

"Feeling?" says Waverhouse.

"Oh yes" says Madam Conk. "That
would go well on a *samisen*."

"If it could be played on the *samisen*, then
it's the real McCoy. Well, how about
these?" asks Waverhouse picking out postcard after postcard.

"Thank you, but I've seen sufficient. For
now at least I know that Coldmoon's not a
strait-laced prude." She thinks she has
achieved some real understanding and appears to have no more queries about Coldmoon, for she remarks "I'm sorry to have
troubled you. Please do not report my visit
to Mr. Coldmoon." Her request reflects
her selfish nature in that she seems to feel
entitled to make a thorough investigation of
Coldmoon whilst expecting that none of her
activities should be revealed to him. Both
Waverhouse and my master concede a half-
hearted "Y-es.": but as Madam Conk gets
up to leave, she consolidates their assent by
saying "I shall, of course, at some later date
repay you for your services."

The two men showed her out and, as they
resumed their seats, Waverhouse exclaimed

"What on earth is that?" At the very same moment my master also ejaculated "Whatever's that?" I suppose my master's wife could not restrain her laughter any longer, for we heard her gurgling in the inner-room.

Waverhouse thereupon addressed her in a loud voice through the sliding door. "That, Mrs. Sneaze, was a remarkable specimen of all that is conventional, of all that is 'common or garden.' But when such characteristics become developed to that incredible degree the result is positively staggering. Such quintessence of the common approximates to the unique. Don't seek to restrain yourself. Laugh to your heart's content."

With evident disgust my master speaks in tones of the deepest revulsion. "To begin with," he says, "her face is unattractive."

Waverhouse immediately takes the cue. "And that nose, squatting, as it were, in the middle of that phiz, seems affectedly unreal."

"Not only that; it's crooked."

"Hunch-backed, one might say. A hunch-backed nose! Quite extraordinary." And Waverhouse laughs in genuine delight.

"It is the face of a woman who keeps her husband under her bottom." My master still looks resentful.

"It is a sort of physiognomy that, left unsold in the nineteenth century, becomes in the twentieth shop-soiled." Waverhouse produces another of his invariably bizarre remarks. At which juncture my master's wife emerges from the inner-room and, being a woman and thus aware of the ways of women, quietly warns them "If you talk such scandal, the rickshaw-owner's wife will snitch on you again."

"But, Mrs. Sneaze, to hear such tattle will do that Goldfield woman no end of good."

"But it's self-demeaning to calumniate a person's face. No one sports that sort of nose as a matter of choice. Besides, she is a woman. You're going a little too far." Her defense of the nose of Madam Conk is simultaneously an indirect defense of her own indifferent looks.

"We're not unkind at all. That creature isn't a woman. She's just an oaf. Waverhouse, am I not right?"

"Maybe an oaf, but a formidable character nonetheless. She gave you quite a tousling, didn't she just?"

"What does she take a teacher for, anyway?"

"She ranks a teacher on roughly the same level as a rickshaw-owner. To earn the respect of such viragoes one needs to have at least a doctor's degree. You were ill-advised not to have taken your doctorate. Don't you agree, Mrs. Sneaze?" Waverhouse looks at her with a smile.

"A doctorate? Quite impossible." Even his wife despairs of my master.

"You never know. I might become one, one of these days. You mustn't always doubt my worth. You may well be ignorant of the fact, but in ancient times a certain Greek, Isocrates, produced major literary works at the age of ninety-four. Similarly,

Sophocles was almost a centenarian when he shook the world with his masterpiece. Simonides was writing wonderful poetry in his eighties. I, too, . . ."

"Don't be silly. How can you possibly expect, you with your stomach troubles, to live that long." Mrs. Sneaze has already determined my master's span of life.

"How dare you! Just go and talk to Dr. Amaki. Anyway it's all your fault. It's because you make me wear this crumpled black cotton surcoat and this patched-up kimono that I am despised by women like Mrs. Goldfield. Very well then. From tomorrow I shall rig myself out in such fineries as Waverhouse is wearing. So get them ready."

"You may well say 'get them ready' but we don't possess any such elegant clothes. Anyway, Mrs. Goldfield only grew civil to Waverhouse after he'd mentioned his uncle's name. Her attitude was in no way conditioned by the ill-condition of your kimono." Mrs. Sneaze has neatly dodged the charge against her.

The mention of that uncle appears to trigger my master's memory, for he turns to Waverhouse and says, "That was the first I ever heard of your uncle. You never spoke of him before. Does he, in fact, exist?"

Waverhouse has obviously been expecting this question, and he jumps to answer it. "Yes, that uncle of mine, a remarkably stubborn man. He, too, is a survival from

"You do say the quaintest things. Where does this uncle live?" asks Mr. Sneaze with a titter.

"In Shizuoka. But he doesn't just live. He lives with a top-knot still on his head. Can you beat it? When we suggest he should wear a hat, he proudly answers that he has never found the weather cold enough to don such gear. And when we hint that he might be wise to stay abed when the weather's freezing, he replies that four hour's sleep is sufficient for any man. He is convinced that to sleep more than four hours is sheer extravagance, so he gets up while it's still pitch-dark. It is his boast that it took many long years of training so to minimize his sleeping hours. 'When I was young,' he says, 'it was indeed hard because I felt sleepy, but recently I have at last achieved that wonderful condition where I can sleep or wake, anywhere, anytime, just as I happen to wish.' It is of course natural that a man of sixty-seven should need less sleep. It has nothing to do with early training, but my uncle is happy in the belief that he has succeeded in attaining his present condition entirely as a result of rigorous self-discipline. And when he goes out, he always carries an iron fan."

"Whatever for?" asks my master.

"I haven't the faintest idea. He just carries it. Perhaps he prefers a fan to a walking stick. As a matter of fact an odd thing happened only the other day." Waverhouse speaks to Mrs. Sneaze.

"Ah yes?" she noncommittally responds.

"In the spring this year he wrote to me out of the blue with a request that I should send him a bowler hat and a frock-coat. I was somewhat surprised and wrote back asking for further clarification. I received an answer stating that the old man himself intended to wear both items on the occasion of the Shizuoka celebration of the war victory, and that I should therefore send them quickly. It was an order. But the quaintness of his letter was that it enjoined me 'to choose a hat of suitable size and, as for the suit, to go and order one from Daimaru of whatever size you think appropriate.'"

"Can one get suits made at Daimaru?"

"No. I think he'd got confused and meant to say at Shirokiya's."

"Isn't it a little unhelpful to say 'of whatever size you think appropriate'?"

"That's just my uncle all over."

"What did you do?"

"What could I do? I ordered a suit which I thought appropriate and sent it him."

"How very irresponsible! And did it fit?"

"More or less, I think. For I later noticed in my home-town newspaper that the venerable Mr. Makiyama had created something of a sensation by appearing at the said celebration in a frock-coat carrying, as usual, his famous iron fan."

"When he's buried, I shall ensure that the fan is placed within the coffin."

"Still it was fortunate that the coat and bowler fitted him."

"But they didn't. Just when I was congratulating myself that everything had gone off smoothly, a parcel came from Shizuoka. I opened it expecting some token of his gratitude, but it proved only to contain the bowler. An accompanying letter stated 'Though you have taken the trouble of making this purchase for me, I find the hat too large. Please be so kind as to take it back to the hatter's and have it shrunk. I will of course defray your consequent expenses by postal order.' "

"Peculiar, one must admit." My master seems greatly pleased to discover that there is someone even more peculiar than himself. "So what did you do?" he asks.

"What did I do? I could do nothing. I'm wearing the hat myself."

"And is that the very hat?" says my master with a smirk.

"And he's a Baron?" asks my master's wife from her mystification.

"Is who?"

"Your uncle with the iron fan."

"Oh, no. He's a scholar of the Chinese classics. When he was young he studied at that shrine dedicated to Confucius in Yushima and became so absorbed in the teachings of Chu-Tzu that, most reverentially, he continues to wear a top-knot in these days of the electric light. There's nothing one can do about it." Waverhouse rubs his chin.

"But I have the impression that in speaking just now to that awful woman you mentioned a Baron Makiyama."

"Indeed you did. I heard you quite distinctly, even in the other room." Mrs. Sneaze for once supports her husband.

"Oh, did I?" Waverhouse permits himself a snigger. "Fancy that. Well, it wasn't true. Had I a Baron for an uncle I would by now be a senior civil servant." Waverhouse is not in the least embarrassed.

"I thought it was somehow queer," says my master with an expression half-pleased, half-worried.

"It's astonishing how calmly you can lie. I must say you're a past master at the game." Mrs. Sneaze is deeply impressed.

"You flatter me. That woman quite outclasses me."

"I don't think she could match you."

"But, Mrs. Sneaze, my lies are merely tarrydiddles. That woman's lies, every one of them, have hooks inside them. They're tricky lies. Lies loaded with malice aforethought. They are the spawn of craftiness. Please never confuse such calculated monkey-minded wickedness with my heaven-sent taste for the comicality of things. Should such confusion prevail, the God of Comedy would have no choice but to weep for mankind's lack of perspicacity."

"I wonder," says my master, lowering his eyes; while Mrs. Sneaze, still laughing, remarks that it all comes down to the same thing in the end.

Up till now I have never so much as crossed the road to investigate the block opposite. I have never clapped eyes on the Goldfield's corner residence so I naturally have no idea what it looks like. Indeed today is the first time that I've even heard of its existence. No one in this house has ever previously talked about a businessman and consequently I, who am my master's cat, have shared his total disinterest in the world of business and his equally total indifference to businessmen. However, having just been present during the colloquy with Madam Conk, having overheard her talk, having imagined her daughter's beauty and charm, and also having given some thought to that family's wealth and power, I have come to realize that, though no more than a cat, I should not idle all my days away lying on the veranda. Nor only that. I cannot help but feel deep sympathy with Coldmoon. His opponent has already bribed a doctor's wife, bribed the wife of the rickshaw-owner, bribed even that high-falutin' mistress of the two-stringed harp. She has so spied upon poor Coldmoon that even his broken teeth have been disclosed; while he has done no more than fiddle with the fastenings of his surcoat and, on occasion, grin. He is guileless even for a bachelor of science just out of the university. And it's not just anyone who can cope with a

woman equipped with such a jut of nose.
My master not only lacks the heart for dealing with matters of this sort, but he lacks the
money too. Waverhouse has sufficient money,
but is such an inconsequential being that
he'd never go out of his way merely to help
Coldmoon. How isolated, then, is that un-
fortunate person who lectures on the mechanics of hanging. It would be less than fair if I
failed at least to try and insinuate myself into
the enemy fortress and, for Coldmoon's sake,
pick up news of their activities. Though but
a cat, I am not quite as other cats. I differ
from the general run of idiot cats and stupid
cats. I am a cat that lodges in the house of a
scholar who, having read it, can bang down
any book by Epictetus on his desk. Con-
centrated in the tip of my tail there is sufficient of the spirit of chivalry for me to take it
upon myself to venture upon knight-errantry.
It is not that I am in any way beholden to
poor Coldmoon, nor am I engaging in fool-
hardy action for the sake of any single individual. If I may be allowed to blow my own
trumpet, I am proposing to take magnificent
unself-interested action simply in order to
realize the will of Heaven that smiles upon
impartiality and blesses the happy medium.
Since Madam Conk makes impermissible use
of such things as the happenings at Azuma
Bridge; since she hires underlings to spy and
eavesdrop on us; since she triumpantly re-
tails to all and sundry the products of her
espionage; since by the employment of rick-

shaw-folk, mere grooms, plain rogues, student riff-raff, crone daily-help, midwives,
witches, masseurs and other trouble-makers
she seeks to trouble a man of talent; for all
these reasons even a cat must do what can be
done to prevent her getting away with it.

The weather, fortunately, is fine. The
thaw is something of nuisance, but one must
be prepared to sacrifice one's life in the cause
of justice. If my feet get muddy and stamp
plum blossom patterns on the veranda, O-
San may be narked but that won't worry me.
For I have come to the superlatively courage-
ous firm decision that I will not put off until
tomorrow what needs to be done today.
Accordingly I whisk off round to the kitchen:
but, having arrived there, pause for further
thought. "Softly, softly," I say to myself.
It's not simply that I've attained the highest
degree of evolution that can occur in cats, but
I make bold to believe my brain is as well-
developed as that of any boy in his third year
at a middle school. Nevertheless, alas, the
construction of my throat is still only that of
a cat, and I cannot therefore speak the babbles of mankind. Thus, even if I succeed in
sneaking into the Goldfield's citadel and there
discovering matters of moment, I shall remain unable to communicate my discoveries
to that Coldmoon who so needs them.
Neither shall I be able to communicate my
gleanings to my master or to Waverhouse.
Such incommunicable knowledge would, like
a buried diamond, be denied its brilliance

and my hard-won wisdom would all be won for nothing. Which would be stupid. Perhaps I should scrap my plan. So thinking, I hesitated on the very doorstep.

But to abandon a project half-way through breeds a kind of regret, that sense of unfulfillment which one feels when the shower one had so confidently expected drifts away under inky clouds into some other part of the countryside. Of course, to persist when one is in the wrong is an altogether different matter; but to press on for the sake of so-called justice and humanity, even at the risk of death uncrowned by success, that, for a man who knows his duty, can be a source of the deepest satisfaction. Accordingly, to engage in fruitless effort and to muddy one's paws on a fool's errand would seem about right for a cat. Since it is my misfortune to have been born a cat, I cannot by turns of the tip of my tail convey, as I can to cats, my thinking to such scholars as Coldmoon, Sneaze and Waverhouse. However, by virtue of felinity, I can, better than all such bookmen, make myself invisible. To do what no one else can do is, of itself, delightful. That I alone should know the inner workings of the Goldfield household is better than that nobody should know. Though I cannot pass my knowledge on, it is still cause for delight that I may make the Goldfields conscious that someone knows their secrets. In the light of this succession of delightful-

I make bold to believe my brain is as well-
All right then. I will go.

Coming to the side-street in the opposite block, there, sure enough, I find a Western-style house dominating the cross-roads as if owned the whole area. Thinking that the master of such a house must be no less stuck-up than his building, I slide past the gate and examine the edifice. Its construction has no merit. Its two stories rear up into the air for no purpose whatever but to impress, even to coerce, the passers-by. This, I suppose, is what Waverhouse means when he calls things common-or-garden. I slink through some bushes, take note of the main entrance to my right, and so find my way round to the kitchen. As might be expected, the kitchen is large: at least ten times as large as that in my master's dwelling. Everything is in such apple-pie order, all so clean and shining, that it cannot be less splendid than that fabulous kitchen of Count Ōkuma so fulsomely described in a recent product of the national press. I tell myself, as I slip inside on silent muddy paws, that this must be "a model kitchen." On the plastered part of its floor the wife of the rickshaw-owner is standing in earnest discussion with a kitchen-maid and a rickshaw-runner. Realizing the dangers of this situation, I hide behind a water-tub.

"That teacher, doesn't he really even know our master's name?" the kitchen-maid demands.

"Of course he knows it. Anyone in this district who doesn't know the Goldfield residence must be a deaf cripple without eyes," snaps the man who pulls the Goldfield's private rickshaw.

"Well, you never know. That teacher's one of those cranks who know nothing at all except what it says in books. If he knew even the least little thing about Mr. Goldfield he might be scared out of his wits. But he hasn't the wits to be scared out of. Why," snorts Blacky's bloody-minded mistress, "he doesn't even know the ages of his own mismanaged children."

"So he's not afraid of our Mr. Goldfield! What a cussed clot he is! There's no call to show him the least consideration. Let's go round and give him something to be scared about."

"Good idea! He says such dreadful things. He was telling his crackpot cronies that, since Madam's nose is far too big for her face, he finds her unattractive. No doubt he thinks himself a proper picture, but his mug's the spitting image of a terra-cotta badger. What can be done, I ask you, with such an animal?"

"And it isn't only his face. The way he saunters down to the public bathhouse carrying a hand-towel is far too high and mighty. He thinks he's the cat's whiskers." My master Sneaze seems notably unpopular, even with this kitchen-maid.

"Let's all go and call him names as loud as we can from just outside his hedge."

"But we mustn't let ourselves be seen.
We must spoil his studying just with shouting,
getting him riled as much as we can.   Those
are Madam's latest orders."

"I know all that" says the rickshaw wife in
a voice that makes it clear that she's only too
ready to undertake one third of their scur-
rilous assignment.   Thinking to myself "So
that's the gang who're going to ridicule my
master," I drift quietly past the noisesome
trio and penetrate yet further into the enemy
fortress.

Cat's paws are as if they do not exist.
Wheresoever they may go, they never make
clumsy noises.   Cats walk as if on air, as if
they trod the clouds, as quietly as a stone
gong light-tapped under water, as an ancient
Chinese harp touched in a sunken cave.   The
walking of a cat is the instinctive realization
of all that is most delicate.   For such as I
this vulgar Western house simply is not there.
Nor do I take cognizance of the rick-
shaw-woman, manservant, kitchen-maids, the
daughter of the house, Madam Conk, her
parlor-maids or even her ghastly husband.
For me they do not exist.   I go where I like
and I listen to whatever talk it interests me to
hear.   Thereafter, sticking out my tongue
and frisking my tail, I walk home self-com-
posedly with my whiskers proudly stiff.   In
this particular field of endeavor there's not
a cat in all Japan so gifted as am I.   Indeed,
I sometimes think I really must be blood-kin
to that monster cat one sees in ancient picture

books. They say that every toad carries in
its forehead a gem that in the darkness
utters light; but packed within my tail I carry
not only the power of God, Buddha, Confucius, Love and even Death but also an in-
infallible panacea for all ills that could be-
witch the entire human race. I can as easily
move unnoticed through the corridors of
Goldfield's awful mansion as a giant god of
stone could squash a milk-blancmange.

At this point, I become so impressed by
my own powers and so conscious of the re-
verence I consequently owe to my own most
precious tail that I feel unable to withhold
immediate recognition of its divinity. I
desire to pray for success in war by worship-
ing my honored Great Tail Gracious
Deity: so I lower my head a little, only to
find I am not facing in the right direction.
When I make the three appropriate obei-
sances I should, of course, as far as it is
possible, be facing toward my tail. But as
I turn my body to fulfill that requirement,
my tail moves away from me. In an effort to
catch up with myself, I twist my neck. But
still my tail eludes me. Being a thing so
sacred, containing as it does the entire uni-
verse in its three-inch length, my tail is
inevitably beyond my power to control. I
spun round in pursuit of it seven and a half
times but, feeling quite exhausted, I finally
gave up. I feel a trifle giddy. For a
moment I lose all sense of where I am and,
deciding that my whereabouts are totally
unimportant, I start to walk about at random.

Then I hear the voice of Madam Conk. It comes from the far side of a paper-window. My ears prick up in sharp diagonals and, once more fully alert, I hold my breath. This is the place which I set out to find.

"He's far too cocky for a penny-pinching usher," she's screaming in that parrot's voice.

"Sure, he's a cocky fellow. I'll have a bit of the bounce taken out of him, just to teach him a lesson. There are one or two fellows I know, fellows from my own province, teaching at his school."

"What fellows are those?"

"Well, there's Tsuki Pinsuke and Fukuchi Kishago for a start. I'll arrange with them for him to be ragged in class."

I don't know from what province old man Goldfield comes, but I'm rather surprised to find it stiff with such outlandish names.

"Is he a teacher of English?" her husband asks.

"Yes. According to the wife of the rick-shaw-owner, his teaching specializes in an English Reader or something like that."

"In any case, he gotta be a rotten teacher."

I'm also struck by the vulgarity of that "gotta be" phraseology.

"When I saw Pinsuke the other day he mentioned that there was some crackpot at his school. When asked the English word for *bancha*, this fathead answered that the English called it, not 'coarse tea' as they actually do, but 'savage tea.' He's now the laughing stock of all his teaching colleagues. Pinsuke added that all the other teachers suffer for this one's follies. Very likely it's the self-same loon."

"It's bound to be. He's got the face you'd expect on a fool who thinks that tea can be savage. And to think he has the nerve to sport such a dashing mustache!"

"Saucy bastard."

If whiskers establish sauciness, every cat is impudent.

"As for that man Waverhouse—Staggering Drunk I'd call him—he's an obstreperous freak if ever I saw one. Baron Makiyama, his uncle indeed! I was sure that no one with a face like his could have a baron for an uncle."

"You, too, are at fault for believing anything which a man of such dubious origins might say."

"Maybe I was at fault. But really there's a limit and he's gone a lot too far." Madam Conk sounds singularly vexed. The odd thing is that neither mentions Coldmoon. I wonder if they concluded their discussion about him before I sneaked up on them or whether perhaps they had earlier decided to block his marriage suit and had therefore already forgotten all about him. I remain disturbed about this question, but there's nothing I can do about it. For a little while I lay crouched down in silence but then I heard a bell ring at the far end of the corridor. What's up down there? Determined this time not to be late on the scene, I set out smartly in the direction of the sound.

I arrived to find some female yattering

away by herself in a loud unpleasant voice.

Since her tones resemble those of Madam Conk, I deduce that this must be that darling daughter, that delicious charmer for whose sake Coldmoon has already risked death by drowning. Unfortunately the paper-windows between us make it impossible for me to observe her beauty and I cannot therefore be sure whether she, too, has a massive nose plonked down in the center of her face. But I infer from her mannerisms, such as the way she sounds to be turning up her nose when she talks, that that organ is unlikely to be an inconspicuous pug-nose. Though she talks continuously, nobody seems to be answering; and I deduce that she must be using one of those modern telephones.

"Is that the Yamato? I want to reserve, for tomorrow, the third box in the lower gallery. All right? Got it? What's that? You can't? But you must. Why should I be joking? Don't be such a fool. Who the devil are you? Chōkichi? Well, Chōkichi, you're not doing very well. Ask the proprietress to come to the phone. What's that? Did you say you were able to cope with any possible inquiries? How dare you speak to me like that? D'you know who I am? This is Miss Goldfield speaking. Oh, you're well aware of that, are you? You really are a fathead. Don't you understand, this is *the* Goldfield. Again? You thank us for being regular patrons? I don't want your stupid thanks. I want the third box in the lower gallery. Don't laugh, you idiot. You must be terribly stupid. You are, you say? If you don't stop being insolent, I shall just ring off. You understand? I can promise you you'll be sorry. Hello. Are you still there? Hello, hello. Speak up. Answer me. Hello, hello, hello." Chōkichi seems to have hung up, for no answer is forthcoming. The girl is now in something of a tizzy and she grinds away at the telephone-handle as though she's gone off her head. A lapdog somewhere round her feet suddenly starts to yap and, realizing I'd better keep my wits about me, I quickly hop off the veranda and creep in under the house.

Just then I hear approaching footsteps and the sound of a paper-door being slid aside. I tilt my head to listen.

"Your father and mother are asking for you, Miss." It sounds like a parlor-maid.

"So who cares?" was the vulgar answer.

"They sent me to fetch you because they've something they want to tell you."

"You're being a nuisance. I said I just don't care." She snubs the maid once more.

"They said it's something to do with Mr. Coldmoon." The maid tries tactfully to put this young vixen into a better humor.

"I couldn't care less if they want to talk about Coldmoon or Piddlemoon. I abominate that man with his daft face looking like a bewildered gourd." Her third sour outburst is directed at the absent Coldmoon. "Hello," she suddenly goes on, "when did you start dressing your hair in the Western style?"

as briefly as she can "Today."

"What sauce. A mere parlor-maid, what's
more." Her fourth attack comes in from a
different direction. "And isn't that a brandnew collar you've got on?"

"Yes, it's the one you gave me recently.
I've been keeping it in my box because it
seemed too good for the likes of me; but my
other collar became so grubby I thought I'd
make the change."

"When did I give it you?"

"It was January you bought it. At
Shirokiya's. It's got the ranks of sumō-
wrestlers set out as decoration on the greeny-
brown material. You said it was too somber
for your style. So you gave it me."

"Did I? Well, it certainly looks nice on
you. How very provoking!"

"I'm much obliged!"

"I didn't intend a compliment. I'm very
much put out."

"Yes, Miss."

"Why did you accept something which so
very much becomes you without letting me
know that it would?"

"But Miss. . ."

"Since it looks that nice on you, it couldn't
fail, could it, to look more nice on me?"

"I'm sure it would have looked delightful
on you."

"Then why didn't you say so? Instead of
that, you just stand there wearing it when you
know I'd like it back. You little beast."
Her vituperations seem to have no end. I

was wondering what would happen when, from the room at the other end of the house, old man Goldfield himself suddenly roared out for his daughter. "Opula," he bellowed. "Opula, come here." She had no choice but to obey and mooched sulkily out of the room containing the telephone. Her lapdog, slightly bigger than myself with its eyes and mouth all bunched together in the middle of its revolting mug, slopped along behind her.

Thereupon, with my usual stealthy steps, I tiptoed back to the kitchen and, through the kitchen-door, found my way to the street. And so back home. My expedition has been notably successful.

Coming thus suddenly from a beautiful mansion to our dirty little dwelling, I felt as though I had descended from a sunlit mountain-top to some dark dismal grot. Whilst on my spying mission, I'd been far too busy to take any notice of the ornaments in the rooms, of the decoration of the sliding-doors and paper-windows or of any similar features; but as soon as I returned and became conscious of the shabbiness of home, I found myself yearning for what Waverhouse claims to despise. I am inclined to think that, after all, there's a good deal more to a businessman than there is to a teacher. Uncertain of the soundness of this thinking, I consult my infallible tail. The oracle confirms that my thinking is correct.

I am surprised to find Waverhouse still sitting in my master's room. His cigarette-stubs, stuffed into the brazier, make it look like a beehive. Comfortably cross-legged on the floor, he is, as usual, talking. It appears, moreover, that during my absence Coldmoon has dropped in. My master, his head pillowed on his arms, lies flat on his back rapt in contemplation of the pattern of the rain-marks on the ceiling. It is another of those meetings of hermits in a peaceful reign.

"Coldmoon, my dear fellow, I seem to remember that you insisted upon maintaining as the darkest of dark secrets the name of that young lady who called your name from the depths of her delirium. But surely the time has now come when you could reveal her identity?" Waverhouse begins to niggle Coldmoon.

"Were it just solely my concern, I wouldn't mind telling you; but since any such disclosure might compromise the other party..."

"So you still won't tell?"

"Besides, I promised the Doctor's wife. . ."

"Promised never to tell anyone?"

"Yes," says Coldmoon back at his usual fiddling with the strings of his surcoat. The strings are a bright purple, objects of a color one could never nowadays find in any shop.

"The color of those strings is early nineteenth century" remarks my supine master. He is genuinely quite indifferent to anything that concerns the Goldfields.

"Quite. It couldn't possibly belong to these times of the Russo-Japanese War. That kind of string would be appropriate only to the garments worn by the rank and file of soldiers under the Shogunate. It is said that on the occasion of his marriage, nearly four hundred years ago, Oda Nobunaga dressed his hair back in the fashion of a tea-whisk; and I have no doubt his projecting top-knot was bound with precisely such a string." Waverhouse goes, as usual, all round the houses to make his little point.

"As a matter of fact, my grandfather wore these strings at the time, not forty years back, when the Tokugawa were putting down the last rebellion before the restoration of the Emperor." Coldmoon takes it all dead seriously.

"Isn't it then about time you presented those strings to a museum? For that well-known lecturer on the mechanics of hanging, that leading bachelor of science, Mr. Avalon Coldmoon to go around looking like a relic of mediaevalism would scarcely help his reputation."

"I myself would be only too ready to follow your advice. However, there's a certain person who says that these strings do specially become me. . ."

"Who on earth could have made such an imperceptive comment?" asks my master in a loud voice as he rolls over onto his side.

"A person not of your acquaintance."

"Never mind that. Who was it?"

"A certain lady."

"Gracious me, what delicacy! Shall I guess who it is? I think it's the lady who whimpered for you from the bottom of the Sumida River. Why don't you tie up your surcoat with those nice purple strings and go on out and get drowned again?" Waverhouse offers a helpful suggestion.

Coldmoon laughs at the sally. "As a matter of fact she no longer calls me from the river-bed. She is now, as it were, in the Pure Land, a little northwest from here. . . "

"Don't hope for too much purity. That ghastly nose looks singularly unwholesome."

"Eh?" says Coldmoon, looking puzzled.

"The Archnose from over the way has just been round to see us. Yes, right here. I can tell you we had quite a surprise. Hadn't we, Sneaze?"

"We had" replies my master still lying on his side but now sipping tea.

"Whom do you mean by the Archnose?"

"We mean the honorable mother of your ever-darling lady."

"Oh!"

"A woman calling herself Mrs. Goldfield came round here asking all sorts of questions about you." My master, clarifying the situation, speaks quite seriously.

I watch poor Coldmoon, wondering if he will be surprised or pleased or embarrassed; but in fact he looks exactly as he always does. And in his accustomed quiet tones he comments "I suppose she's asking if I'll marry the daughter? Was that it?"; and he goes on twisting and untwisting his purple strings.

"Far from it! That mother happens to

own the most enormous nose..." But before Waverhouse could finish his sentence my master interrupted him with a sudden irrelevance.

"Listen," he chirps, "I've been trying to compose a new-style *haiku* on that snout of hers." Mrs. Sneaze begins to giggle in the next room.

"You're taking it all extremely lightly! And have you composed your poem?"

"I've made a start. The first line goes 'A Conker Festival takes place in this face.'"

"And then?"

"'At which one offers sacred wine.'"

"And the concluding line?"

"I've not yet got to that."

"Interesting" says Coldmoon with a grin.

"How about this for the missing line?" improvises Waverhouse. "'Two orifices dim.'"

Whereupon Coldmoon offers "'So deep no hairs appear.'"

They were thus thoroughly enjoying themselves by proposing wilder and wilder lines when from the street beyond the hedge came the voices of several people shouting "Where's that terra-cotta badger? Come on out, you terra-cotta badger. Terra-cotta badger! Yah!"

Both my master and Waverhouse look somewhat startled and they peer out through the hedge. Loud hoots of derisive laughter are followed by the sound of footsteps running away.

"Whatever can they mean by a terra-cotta

badger?" Waverhouse asks in puzzled tones.

"I've no idea" replies my master.

"An unusual occurrence" says Coldmoon.

Waverhouse suddenly gets to his feet as if he had remembered something. "For some several lustra," he declaims in parody of the style of public lecturers, "I have devoted myself to the study of aesthetic nasofrontology and I would accordingly now like to trespass on your time and patience in order to present certain interim conclusions at which I have arrived." His initiative has been so suddenly taken that my master just stares up at him in silent blank amazement.

Coldmoon's tiniest voice observes "I'd love to hear your interim conclusions."

"Though I have made a thorough study of this matter, the origin of the nose remains, alas, still deeply obfuscated. The first question that arises reflects the assumption that the nose is intended for use. The functional approach. If that premiss be valid, would not two mere vent-holes meet the case? There is no obvious need either for such arrogant protusion or for the nasal arrogation of a median position in the human physiognomy. Why then should the nasal organ thus," and he paused to pinch his own, "thrust itself forward?"

"Yours doesn't stick out much," cut in my master rather rudely.

"At any rate it has no indentations, no incurvations; still less could it be described as countersunk or infundibular. I draw your attention to these facts because if you fail to make the necessary distinction between having two holes in the medio-frontal area of the face and having two such holes in some form of protuberance, you will inevitably be unable to follow the quintessential drift of my dissertation. Now, it is at least my own, albeit humble, opinion that it is by an accumulation of human actions trifling in themselves, for who could attach major importance to the blowing of one's nose, that the organ in question has developed into its present phenomenal form."

"How very humbly you do hold your humble views" interjects my master.

"As you will know, the act of blowing the nose involves the coarctation of that organ. Such stenosis of the nose, such astrictive and, one might even venture to say, pleonastic stimulation of so localized an area results, by response to that stimulus and in accordance with the well-established principles of Lamarckian evolutionary theory, in the development of that specific area to a degree disproportionate to the development of other areas. The epidermis of the affected area inevitably indurates and the subcutaneous material so coagulates as eventually to ossify."

"That's a bit extreme. Surely you can't turn flesh to bone just by blowing your nose." Coldmoon, as behoves a bachelor of science, lodges a protest. Waverhouse continues to deliver his speech with the utmost nonchalance.

"I can well appreciate your natural dubieties, but the proof of the pudding remains in the eating. For, behold, there is bone there; and that bone has demonstrably been molded. Nevertheless and despite that bone, one snivels. If one snivels one has to blow the nose, and in the course of that action both sides of the bone get worn away until the nose itself acquires the shape of a high and narrow bulge. It is indeed a terrifying process. But just as little taps of dropping water will eventually bore through granite, so has the high straight ridge of the nasal organ been smithied by incessant nose-blows. Thus painfully was fangled the hard straight line on one's face."

"But yours is flabby."

"I deliberately refrain from any discussion of this particular feature as it may be observed in the physiognomy of the lecturer himself; for such a purely personal approach involves the dangers of self-exculpation, the temptation to gloss over, even to defend, one's individual defects or deficiencies. But the nose of the honorable Mrs. Goldfield is such that I would wish to bring it to your attention as the most highly developed of its kind, the most egregiously rare object, in the world."

Coldmoon cries out in spontaneous admiration. "Hear, hear."

"But anything whatever that develops to an extreme degree becomes thereby intimidating. Even terrifying. Spectacular it may be, but simultaneously awesome, unapproachable. Thus the bridge of that lady's nose, though certainly magnificent, appears to me unduly rigid, unacceptably steep. If one pauses to consider the nature of the noses of the ancients, it seems probable that those of Socrates, Oliver Goldsmith and William Thackeray were strikingly imperfect from the structural point of view; but those very imperfections had their own peculiar charms. This is, no doubt, the intellection behind the saying that a nose, like a mountain, is not significant because it is high but because it is odd. Similarly, the popular catch-phrase that 'dumplings are better than nosegays' is no doubt a corruption of some yet more ancient adage to the effect that dumplings are better than noses. From which it follows that, viewed aesthetically, the nose of Citizen Waverhouse is just about right."

Coldmoon and my master greet this fantastication with peals of appreciative laughter; and even Waverhouse joins in.

"Now, the piece I have just been reciting..."

"Distinguished speaker, I must object to your use of the phrase 'reciting a piece': a somewhat vulgar word one would only expect from a storyteller." Coldmoon, catching Waverhouse in the use of language which only recently Waverhouse had criticized, feels himself revenged.

"In which case, sir, and having with your gracious permission purged myself of error, I would now like to touch upon the matter of the proper proportion between the nose and

its associated face. If I were simply to dis- 213
cuss noses in disregard of their relation to
other entities, then I would declare without
fear of contradiction that the nose of Mrs.
Goldfield is superb, superlative and, though
possibly supervacaneous, one well-placed to
win first prize at any exhibition of nasal development which might be organized by the
long-nosed goblins on Mount Kurama.
But alas! And even alack! That nose
appears to have been formed, fashioned, dare
I say fabricated, without any regard for the
configuration of such other major items as
the eyes and mouth. Julius Caesar was
undoubtedly dowered with a very fine nose.
But what do you think would be the result if
one scissored off that Julian beak and fixed it
on the face of this cat here? Cats' foreheads
are proverbially diminutive. To raise the
tower of Caesar's boned proboscis on such a
tiny site would be like plonking down on a
chessboard the giant image of Buddha now
to be seen at Nara. The juxtaposing of disproportionate elements destroys aesthetic
value. Mrs. Goldfield's nose, like that of
Caesar, is, as a thing in itself, a most dig-
nified and majestic protuberance. But how
does it appear in relation to its surroundings?
Of course those circumjacent areas are not
quite so barren of aesthetic merit as the face
of this cat. Nevertheless it is a bloated face,
the face of an epileptic skivvy whose eye-
brows meet in a sharp-pitched gable above
thin tilted eyes. Gentlemen, I ask you:

what sort of nose could ever survive so lamentable a face?"

As Waverhouse paused, a voice could be heard from the back of the house. "He's still going on about noses. What a spiteful bore he is."

"That's the wife of the rickshaw-owner," my master explains to Waverhouse.

Waverhouse resumes. "It is a great if unexpected honor for this present lecturer to discover at, as it were, the back of the hall an interested listener of the gentle sex. I am especially gratified that a gleam of charm should be added to my arid lecture by the bell-sweet voice of this new participant. It is, indeed, a happiness unlooked for; a serendipity. To be worthy of our beautiful lady's patronage I would gladly alter the academic style of this discourse into a more popular mode; but, as I am just about to discuss a problem in mechanics, the unavoidably technical terminology may prove a trifle difficult for the ladies to comprehend. I must therefore beg them to be patient."

Coldmoon responds to the mention of mechanics with his usual grin.

"The point I wish to establish is that such a nose and such a face will never harmonize. In brief, they cannot conform to Zeising's rule of the Golden Section, a fact which I propose to prove by use of a mechanical formula. We should first designate H as the height of the nose, and α as the angle between the nose and the level surface of the face.

Please note that W is, of course, the weight of the nose. Are you with me thus far?"

"Hardly" breathes my master.

"Coldmoon, what about you?"

"I, too, am slightly at a loss."

"You distress me, Coldmoon. Sneaze doesn't matter, but I'm shocked that you, a bachelor of science, should fail to understand. This formula is a key part of my lecture. To abandon this portion of my argument must render the whole endeavor pointless. However, such things can't be helped. I'll omit the formula and merely deliver the peroration."

"Is there a peroration?" asks my master in genuine curiosity.

"Why, naturally! A lecture without a peroration is like a Western dinner shorn of the dessert. Now, listen, both of you, carefully. I am launching on my peroration. Gentlemen, if one reflects upon the theory which I have advanced on this occasion and gives due weight to the related theories of Virchow and of Wisemen, one is bound also to take appropriate account of the problem of the heredity of congenital form. Furthermore, though there is a substantial body of evidence to support the contention that acquired characteristics are not hereditarily transmissible, one cannot lightly dismiss the view that the mental conditions associated with hereditarily transmissible forms are themselves also transmissible. It is consequently reasonable to assume that a child

born to the possessor of a nose of such enormity will have an abnormal nose. Because
Coldmoon is still young, he has not noticed
any particular abnormality in the structure of
Miss Goldfield's nasal organ. But the genes
lurk. The products of heredity take long to
incubate. One never knows. Perhaps it
would need no more than a sharp change of
climate for the daughter's snout suddenly to
germinate and, in a mere instant, to tumesce
into a replica of that of her most honorable
mother. In sum, I believe that in the light
of my theoretical demonstration, it would
seem prudent to forswear any idea of this
marriage. Now, while it is still possible to
do so. I would go so far as to claim that,
quite apart from the master of this house,
even his monstrous cat asleep among us,
would not dissent from my conclusions."

My master sits up at last. "Of course,"
he says "no one in his senses would ever
marry a daughter of that creature! Really,
my dear Coldmoon," he insists in real earnest,
"you simply must not marry her."

I seek in my own humble way to second all
these sentiments by mewing twice. Coldmoon, however, does not seem to be particularly alarmed. "If you two sages share
that opinion, I would be prepared to give her
up: but it would be cruel if the consequent
distress brought the person in question into
poor health."

"That," burbled Waverhouse happily,
"might even be regarded as a sort of sex-
crime."

Only my master continues to take the matter seriously. "Don't joke about such things. That girl wouldn't wither away, not if she's the daughter of that forward and presumptuous creature who strove to humiliate me from the moment she set an uninvited foot in my house." My master again works himself up into a great huff.

At which point there is a further outbreak of laughter from, by the sound of it, three or four people on the far side of the hedge. A voice says "You're a stuck-up blockhead." Another jeers "I bet you'd like to live in a bigger house." A third loud voice announces "Ain't it a pity! You swagger around but you're only a silly old windbag."

My master goes out on to the veranda and shouts with matching violence "Hold your tongues. What do you think you're doing making this sort of disturbance so close to my property?"

The laughter gets even louder. "Hark at him. It's silly old Savage Tea. Savage Tea. Savage Tea." They set up an abusive chant.

My master, looking furious, turns abruptly, snatches up his stick and rushes out into the street.

Waverhouse claps his hands in pure delight. "Up guards and at 'em" he shouts, urging my master on.

Coldmoon sits and grins, twisting his purple fastening-strings.

I follow my master and, as I crawl out through a gap in the hedge, find him standing in the middle of the street with his stick held awkwardly in his hand. Apart from him, the street is empty. I cannot help but feel that he's been made to make a ninny of himself.

Other Titles in the Tuttle Library

THE PAPER DOOR AND OTHER STORIES *by Shiga Naoya, translated by Lane Dunlop*

THE PORNOGRAPHERS *by Akiyuki Nozaka, translated by Michael Gallagher*

RASHOMON AND OTHER STORIES *by Ryunosuke Akutagawa, translated by Takashi Kojima*

THE RIVER WITH NO BRIDGE *by Sue Sumii, translated by Susan Wilkinson*

ROMAJI DIARY AND SAD TOYS *by Takuboku Ishikawa, translated by Sanford Goldstein and Seishi Shinoda*

THE SAMURAI ETHIC AND MODERN JAPAN: Yukio Mishima on Hagakure *translated by Kathryn Sparling*

SENRYU: Poems of the People *compiled and illustrated by J. C. Brown*

SHANK'S MARE: Japan's Great Comic Novel of Travel and Ribaldry *by Ikku Jippensha, translated by Thomas Satchell*

SHIOKARI PASS *by Ayako Miura, translated by Bill and Sheila Fearnehough*

THE SQUARE PERSIMMON AND OTHER STORIES *by Takashi Atoda, translated by Millicent Horton*

THE TALE OF GENJI: A Reader's Guide *by William J. Puette*

TANGLED HAIR: Selected Tanka from Midaregami *by Akiko Yosano, translated by Sanford Goldstein and Seishi Shinoda*

THE TEN FOOT SQUARE HUT AND TALES OF THE HEIKE: Being Two Thirteenth Century Japanese Classics, the "Hojoki" and Selections from the "Heike Monogatari" *translated by A. L. Sadler*